SPIRIT ANIMALS

Harnessing the Power of
Spirit Guides and Their
Messages

Sarah Ripley

Spirit Animals: Harnessing the Power of Spirit Guides and Their Messages

Other Titles by
Sarah Ripley:

Sabbats and Esbats: A Modern Witch's Guide to Wiccan Rituals

Angel Numbers and Divine Numerology: Unlocking the Meaning and Divine Messages of the Universe

Conjure Your Desires: Rituals, Spells and Runes for Manifesting Your Dreams.

369 Manifesting your Dreams: A Manifestation Journal to Create the Life You Desire

The Shadow Work Journal: A Guide for Exploring your Hidden Self

The Power of the 369 Method: Unlock the Cosmic Code and Create the Life you Desire using the Law of Attraction

Join the Community to Receive Exclusive Bonus Content.

Scan the QR code to receive your FREE 2024 and 2025 Moon Phase Calendars!

Table of Contents

The Origin of Spirit Animals

The concept of spirit animals as guides stretches back into the mists of time, far beyond the realm of written history. We can trace its roots to the practices of ancient hunter-gatherer societies who lived in an intimate relationship with nature. For them, the natural world wasn't just a source of food and shelter, but a realm teeming with spirits. Animals, especially those they hunted, held a particular significance. Imagine our early ancestors, living in close communion with nature, relying on the hunt for survival.

Cave paintings, often depicting animals like bison, deer, and mammoths, are more than just hunting strategies or celebratory trophies. These artworks might be interpreted as a way to connect with the spirit of the sacrificed creature. Imagine our ancestors, deeply aware of the precarious balance between hunter and hunted, acknowledging the life force they were taking. The paintings could be a form of blessing, a plea for continued abundance from the natural world. It could also be a way to express gratitude to the animal spirits, ensuring a harmonious relationship with the source of their sustenance.

The specific animals depicted might hold symbolic meaning. A powerful bison might represent strength and resilience, while a swift deer could symbolize agility and grace. By incorporating these animal spirits into their art, early humans might have been seeking to tap into these qualities for their own survival.

The belief in spirit animals as guides stretches far beyond a single culture or historical period. From the Celts of Europe to the indigenous tribes of North and South America, and across many Asian and African cultures, we find traditions that revere the connection between humans and the animal world. This widespread phenomenon hints at something deeply rooted within us.

This cross-cultural acceptance of spirit animals speaks to a fundamental human connection with the natural world. Throughout history, humans have relied on animals for survival, guidance, and companionship. Animals have been essential for food, clothing, and tools. Observing their behavior offered insights into weather patterns, migration cycles, and hunting strategies. This deep dependence fostered a sense of respect and a recognition of the inherent power and wisdom animals possess.

The concept of spirit animals takes this connection a step further. It suggests that animals can act as personal guides, offering us support and direction on our life paths. By embodying specific traits and qualities, spirit animals can serve as metaphors for the strengths we need to cultivate or the challenges we need to overcome. In essence, these beliefs bridge the gap between the human and animal realms, fostering a sense of kinship and offering a framework for understanding ourselves and the world around us.

As civilizations developed and organized religions emerged, animal symbolism continued to hold a prominent place in spiritual traditions. Across the globe, from ancient Egypt to the Celts of Europe, animals were seen as powerful entities, imbued with symbolic meaning and even worshipped as deities. This deep connection with the natural world laid the foundation for the belief in spirit animals – personal guides with whom humans shared a profound connection.

The belief in spirit animals as guides manifested in a fascinatingly diverse way across cultures. Some traditions held the concept of a singular, lifelong spirit animal. This constant companion existed not only in the physical world, perhaps appearing in dreams or visions, but also in the spiritual realm, offering unwavering support and guidance. For these individuals, the spirit animal was a confidante, a source of unwavering strength, and a source of comfort throughout life's journey. They might view certain animal behaviors as messages or omens from their spirit guide, interpreting these signs to navigate personal challenges.

In other traditions, the relationship with spirit animals was more fluid. People might encounter different animal guides at various stages of their lives, each with a unique set of lessons and strengths to impart. A young warrior might find a powerful bear offering guidance on courage and perseverance, while a woman entering motherhood might connect with a nurturing wolf spirit. This adaptability reflects the ever-changing nature of life itself. As individuals evolve and face new challenges, they might find themselves drawn to different animal spirits whose wisdom resonates with their current needs.

However, regardless of the specifics, a core belief remained constant: animals were seen as repositories of wisdom gleaned from their own existence in the natural world. This wisdom wasn't simply instinctive behavior; it was a deep understanding of life's rhythms, challenges, and triumphs. Humans, through their connection with spirit animals, could tap into this wellspring of knowledge and apply it to their own spiritual journeys. The spirit animal wasn't just a guide; it became a powerful guardian spirit, offering protection from harm, both physical and spiritual. By heeding the insights gleaned from their spirit animal, individuals could navigate life's uncertainties with greater clarity, purpose, and courage.

Even though our modern lives are a far cry from the hunter-gatherer societies of our distant past, the concept of spirit animals continues to hold a powerful allure. In a world increasingly dominated by technology and concrete jungles, the idea of a spiritual connection with the natural world offers a sense of grounding and belonging. It's a way to reconnect with that primal, instinctive part of ourselves – our "inner wildness" – that may feel buried beneath the layers of daily routines and societal expectations.

This reconnection with nature extends beyond simply appreciating the beauty of a sunset or a walk in the woods. The concept of spirit animals allows us to forge a deeper, more personal bond with the natural world. By exploring the symbolism associated with different animals, we can gain valuable insights into our own unique selves. The owl, for instance, might symbolize wisdom and discernment, while the bear represents strength and introspection. If you find yourself particularly drawn to a specific animal, it could be a sign that its spirit resonates with your own inner qualities or the challenges you currently face.

This exploration of animal symbolism isn't just about intellectual understanding; it's a deeply personal journey of self-discovery. By delving into the meaning associated with different creatures, we can gain invaluable insights into our strengths and weaknesses. Perhaps the unwavering focus of a hawk reminds us of the need for determination in pursuing our goals. Or maybe the playful spirit of a dolphin encourages us to embrace a more lighthearted approach to life.

Ultimately, the concept of spirit animals offers a powerful tool for navigating life's path. By recognizing the wisdom embodied by these creatures, we can gain valuable guidance and support on our own journeys. Whether it's facing a difficult decision or simply seeking a deeper understanding of ourselves, the spirit world, as embodied by our animal guides, can offer a source of strength, clarity, and inspiration.

What is a Spirit Animal?

In many indigenous cultures, the concept of a spirit animal transcends the realm of mere symbolism. It's not simply a mascot or a favorite creature you admire, but a powerful guide intricately woven into the fabric of your life's journey. This isn't a domineering force dictating your every step, but rather your spirit animal acts as a wise teacher, revealing valuable lessons through its own unique nature and abilities.

This connection isn't a one-way street. By observing your spirit animal, you gain deeper insight into its world – how it navigates the complexities of its environment, overcomes challenges, and thrives in the face of adversity. Each spirit animal embodies a specific set of strengths, skills, and knowledge honed through its own unique struggles for survival. As you learn about your spirit animal's strengths, a fascinating parallel emerges – valuable insights for your own "Spirit Walk," the spiritual path you travel in life.

Imagine a courageous wolf as your spirit animal. By observing its pack dynamics, hunting strategies, and unwavering loyalty, you might glean lessons in leadership, teamwork, and fierce determination. Perhaps a graceful deer is your guide, teaching you about adaptability, gentleness, and the importance of following your intuition. Every spirit animal offers a unique perspective, a lens through which you can better understand your own strengths, weaknesses, and the path that lies ahead.

The concept of a spirit animal isn't about blind obedience or adhering to a predetermined fate. It's a dynamic dialogue between you and your spirit guide, a source of inspiration and encouragement. By understanding the wisdom embodied by these creatures, you gain valuable guidance and support on your own journey. As you delve deeper into the connection with your spirit animal, you unlock a wellspring of knowledge and insight, empowering you to face challenges with greater clarity, navigate life's uncertainties with courage, and ultimately, walk your unique path with purpose and fulfillment.

The appearance of your spirit animal isn't just a random encounter; it signifies a crucial moment in your life's journey. It's a powerful call to action, a nudge from the universe urging you to connect with your authentic self and embark on the path towards discovering your life's purpose. This doesn't happen through a single, earth-shattering encounter. It's more likely to unfold through a series of seemingly coincidental occurrences.

The key lies in paying close attention. Perhaps you start seeing a particular animal repeatedly – a majestic eagle soaring overhead, a sly fox flitting across your path, or a wise owl perched on a branch outside your window. These recurring encounters aren't random; they're messages from your spirit animal, urging you to delve deeper into its symbolism and the lessons it embodies. Notice any patterns or themes that emerge around these encounters. Does the appearance of your spirit animal coincide with significant life decisions, moments of personal transformation, or periods of self-doubt? By becoming more aware of these connections, you begin to understand the messages woven into the fabric of your everyday experiences.

Imagine you find yourself drawn to the image of a wolf, a creature known for its loyalty, strength, and leadership. If you're facing a challenging decision in your career, the appearance of a wolf might be a sign to tap into your inner strength and leadership qualities. Perhaps you've been neglecting your true passions to pursue a more "stable" path. The wolf's presence could be a nudge to re-evaluate your priorities and reconnect with your authentic desires.

As you develop this heightened awareness, you unlock the ability to decipher the hidden messages embedded in your daily life. The rustling of leaves or the sound of a bird's call can become whispers of guidance from your spirit animal. By learning to interpret these messages, you gain invaluable insights and a renewed sense of purpose. It's through this connection with your spirit animal that you embark on a profound journey of self-discovery, ultimately leading you towards fulfilling your unique potential and walking your life's path with authenticity and clarity.

The communication between you and your spirit animal is a unique and multifaceted dance. Unlike a traditional teacher delivering a lecture, your spirit animal's messages can arrive through a captivating array of channels. Be prepared to receive them in dreams, where vivid imagery and symbolic actions unfold, offering potent insights into your inner world and the challenges you face. Visions, fleeting glimpses of your spirit animal while awake, can also serve as powerful messengers. Pay close attention to the emotions evoked by these visions and the context in which they appear.

The most magical form of communication might be a physical encounter in the natural world. Perhaps you find yourself face-to-face with your spirit animal during a hike in the woods, or a majestic bird circles overhead as you contemplate a difficult decision. These encounters, even if brief, can leave a lasting impression and serve as a powerful reminder of the guidance your spirit animal offers.

The key lies in remaining open to the message, regardless of the form it takes. Don't get caught up in preconceived notions about the animal or how communication "should" happen. Your spirit animal is an intuitive being, perfectly attuned to your specific needs and the lessons you need to learn at that point in your journey. A playful dolphin might appear in a dream to remind you to embrace joy and find lightness in life, even when faced with challenges. Conversely, a seemingly intimidating bear encountered in the wild could symbolize the inner strength you possess, urging you to face your fears and overcome obstacles.

Remember, your spirit animal isn't there to judge or criticize. It's a wise and patient guide, offering support and encouragement through subtle nudges and potent symbols. By cultivating an open mind and a receptive heart, you'll be able to decipher these messages, no matter how they appear. This open-mindedness allows you to receive the guidance you most need, propelling you forward on your path of self-discovery and personal growth.

Unlike a pet or a chosen companion, a spirit animal isn't something you can pick and choose. It's a powerful force that chooses you, entering your life when you're most receptive to its guidance. Trying to force this manifestation through meditation rituals or wishful thinking is futile. The true essence of a spirit animal lies in its ability to appear at a pivotal moment, precisely when you need its wisdom the most.

Imagine yourself standing at a crossroads, unsure of the path to take. You might yearn for a wise counselor to offer direction, a voice to illuminate the possibilities before you. This is precisely the moment when your spirit animal might choose to reveal itself. Perhaps a majestic hawk soars overhead, its keen eyesight mirroring your own need for a broader perspective. Or maybe a wise old owl takes roost on a nearby branch, its presence a reminder to approach the situation with discernment and patience.

The timing of your spirit animal's appearance is no accident. It arrives like a perfectly placed stepping stone, guiding you across a turbulent river of uncertainty. This impeccable timing underscores the profound connection that exists between you and your spirit guide. They are intricately attuned to your life's journey, aware of the challenges you face and the lessons you need to learn. Their arrival isn't a random event but a deliberate intervention, meant to offer support and encouragement as you navigate a critical juncture in your life.

However, this doesn't mean you should remain entirely passive. While forcing a connection isn't productive, there are ways to cultivate a receptiveness to your spirit animal's presence. Opening your mind to the symbolism of the natural world, practicing mindfulness, and quieting the external noise can create a space for your spirit animal to communicate. By embarking on this journey of self-discovery with an open heart and a willingness to learn, you create the fertile ground necessary for your spirit animal to blossom and offer its invaluable guidance.

Totem Animals

The concept of spirit animals can be captivating, but it can also get confusing. Let's break down the difference between spirit animals, totem animals, and power animals to understand how they each play a role in our lives.

In contrast to spirit animals, which offer personal lessons, totem animals serve as powerful protectors and sources of strength. Imagine them as guardian spirits, invoked by individuals or entire tribes to access specific abilities and overcome challenges.

Within many indigenous cultures, particularly those of Native America, social structures extend beyond the tribe itself. Many organize into smaller groups called clans. These clans often have a totem animal, a powerful spirit creature that serves as a sort of founding member or "ancestor" for the group. This totem animal acts as a unifying force, creating a shared connection that binds the clan members together.

The choice of a totem animal is rarely arbitrary. Typically, the totem will be an animal native to the region the tribe inhabits. This fosters a deep connection between the people and their environment. The Great Lakes area, for instance, boasts a rich ecosystem that provided sustenance and inspiration for the indigenous tribes who lived there. Common totems in this region include the wolf, bear, turtle, and deer. Each of these animals carries powerful symbolism that resonates with the tribe's values and way of life.

For example, the wolf, known for its intelligence, leadership skills, and strong pack mentality, might be a totem for a clan that emphasizes cooperation, hunting prowess, and community. The bear, a symbol of strength, resilience, and introspection, could be a totem for a clan that values self-reliance, courage, and the ability to navigate challenging situations. The enduring nature of the turtle, with its slow and steady pace and protective shell, might represent a clan that prioritizes wisdom, patience, and perseverance. Finally, the deer, a creature of grace, swiftness, and keen senses, could be a totem for a clan that values adaptability, resourcefulness, and connection to the natural world.

Within these larger clans, there might exist sub-clans identified with specific variations of the totem animal. For instance, the Turtle Clan might have sub-clans associated with the Snapping Turtle or the Painted Turtle, each carrying unique meanings and attributes. These variations further personalize the totemic connection and emphasize the diverse skillsets within the tribe.

By identifying with a totem animal, clans not only strengthen their bond with each other but also forge a deeper connection with the land they call home. The symbolism of the totem becomes woven into the fabric of the clan's identity, shaping their traditions, values, and even their understanding of the universe.

The "spiritual powers" embodied by the totem animal go far beyond mere symbolism. They act as a source of empowerment, enabling each clan to fulfill a designated role within the tribe. This creates a harmonious and well-functioning social structure.

Take the Turtle Clan, often known as the "Keepers of Wisdom." Their totem, the turtle, embodies not only longevity and stability but also the slow and steady accumulation of knowledge. By drawing upon these qualities, the Turtle Clan leverages their totem's power to safeguard the tribe's cultural heritage. They become the guardians of traditions, stories, and ceremonies, ensuring their transmission to future generations. They might be responsible for educating young members of the tribe, ensuring the continuity of their way of life.

Similarly, a Bear Clan, drawing strength from the totem's symbolism of courage and resilience, might take on the critical role of protecting the tribe from physical threats. The bear's fierce nature and formidable presence translates into a sense of duty for the clan members. They might be the warriors of the tribe, responsible for defending the community during times of conflict. Their training and bravery, inspired by the bear's spirit, ensures the safety and well-being of the entire tribe.

This system of totem-based roles fosters interdependence within the tribe. Each clan, empowered by their unique totem animal, contributes a vital skillset to the larger whole. The Turtle Clan provides the foundation of knowledge, the Bear Clan safeguards the tribe, and other clans, drawing on their own totem's power, might specialize in hunting, healing, or diplomacy. This interconnectedness ensures the tribe's survival and prosperity, showcasing the practical application of the spiritual bond with the animal world.

Unraveling the true essence of a totem animal goes beyond simply recognizing its physical traits. While a majestic wolf might inspire awe with its strength and leadership, and a lumbering bear embodies power and resilience, a totem's significance lies deeper, in the symbolic power it represents.

It's important to look past stereotypical portrayals of animals in popular culture. A seemingly meek creature like the rabbit, often associated with timidity, can be a surprisingly potent totem. In some cultures, the rabbit represents resourcefulness, cunning, and even fertility. These qualities can be immensely valuable for individuals or clans facing challenges that require adaptability, quick thinking, and the ability to thrive in difficult circumstances.

The true power of the totem lies not in the physical prowess of the animal itself, but in the qualities it embodies and how these qualities align with the needs of the individual or tribe. For instance, a tribe facing a period of famine might find immense guidance in a totem like the spider. While not necessarily a physically imposing creature, the spider is a master weaver, symbolizing the ability to create, mend, and adapt. This totem could inspire the tribe to find new sources of sustenance, develop innovative tools, and strengthen their social bonds during a period of hardship.

Ultimately, the most potent totem animal is the one that resonates most deeply. Whether it's a soaring eagle symbolizing freedom and vision, or a wise old owl representing knowledge and discernment, the true power lies in the connection between the symbolic meaning of the animal and the aspirations or challenges of the individual or group it represents.

By understanding the distinct roles of totem animals, we gain a deeper appreciation for the rich tapestry of beliefs and practices within indigenous cultures. These powerful guardians serve as sources of strength, identity, and purpose, ensuring the continuity and well-being of the tribe across generations.

Power Animals

The terms "power animal" and "spirit animal" are often used interchangeably, particularly in modern contexts. However, within some indigenous traditions and shamanic practices, subtle distinctions exist. Both concepts center around the idea of a spiritual connection between humans and the animal world, but they differ in their focus and purpose.

A spirit animal can be understood as a personal guide or companion spirit. It's believed to be an energetic connection with a specific animal that offers guidance, protection, and support throughout your life's journey. This connection can be established through dreams, visions, or simply a deep personal resonance with a particular animal.

The spirit animal reflects your own inner qualities and potential. It might embody strengths you already possess or represent traits you're striving to cultivate. For example, if you're facing a challenge requiring courage, a lion or a bear might appear as your spirit animal, offering you the strength and determination associated with those creatures.

The relationship with your spirit animal is typically long-lasting, potentially enduring throughout your entire life. It's a source of comfort and inspiration, reminding you of your inherent strengths and the path you're meant to walk.

Unlike spirit animals, which offer lifelong guidance and lessons, power animals function as temporary allies. Imagine them as powerful reinforcements, appearing on the battlefield of life precisely when you need a specific set of strengths. These strengths are often tied to the animal's natural characteristics and symbolic associations.

Think of a time when you faced a daunting task, perhaps a challenging presentation at work or a difficult personal decision. You might feel a sudden connection to an animal known for its courage and determination, like a lion or a hawk. This isn't a coincidence; it's your power animal emerging to offer a temporary boost of those very qualities. These power animals can manifest in various ways, appearing in dreams, visions, or even through a chance encounter with the physical animal. Their presence serves as a potent reminder that you possess the strength and determination to overcome the obstacle before you.

The relationship with a power animal is dynamic and ever-evolving. It's not a permanent bond, but rather a temporary alliance forged to address a specific challenge. Once you've navigated the obstacle and the qualities offered by the power animal are no longer as crucial, the connection might fade. This doesn't diminish the significance of their support; it simply signifies that the lesson has been learned, and the strength has been integrated into your own being.

However, the lessons imparted by power animals can have lasting effects. By drawing strength from these temporary allies, you gain a deeper understanding of your own inner potential. The courage of the lion or the focus of the hawk becomes a part of your personal repertoire, a resource you can tap into when faced with future challenges. Power animals serve as a source of inspiration, reminding you of the strength and resilience you possess within yourself.

In essence, power animals act as temporary guides, offering targeted support during critical junctures in your life. By recognizing their presence and embracing the qualities they embody, you navigate challenges with greater fortitude and emerge from them a little wiser and stronger.

Finding Your Spirit Animal

In the vast tapestry of spiritual beliefs, the concept of a spirit animal holds a powerful allure. This personal guide, unlike a chosen companion, appears when you're most receptive to its wisdom. Unveiling your spirit animal isn't a singular, earth-shattering event, but rather a journey of exploration and self-discovery. Here, we delve into various methods to connect with this potent force, from venturing into the wilderness on a Spirit Walk to the quiet contemplation of meditation. Through these practices, you can embark on a path of personal growth, fostering a deeper understanding of yourself and the spirit animal that walks beside you.

Immersing yourself in nature is a powerful way to connect with your spirit animal. This approach honors the deep connection between humans and the natural world, the very foundation of the spirit animal concept. By stepping away from the hustle and bustle of daily life and entering a wild space, you open yourself to the possibility of encountering your spirit guide.

There's a certain magic to simply being present in nature. Go for hikes in local forests, embark on camping trips under a canopy of stars, or even find a quiet corner in a nearby park. As you spend time outdoors, become an observer. Pay close attention to the wildlife around you. Notice any animals that seem to draw your attention, those that linger in your gaze a little longer than others. Perhaps you find yourself repeatedly encountering a particular bird species on your walks, or a majestic deer grazes near your campsite, seemingly unafraid. These encounters may not be random occurrences but subtle nudges from the spirit world.

Once you've identified an animal that piques your curiosity, observe its behavior. Watch how it moves, interacts with its environment, and communicates with other creatures of its kind. Is it a solitary creature radiating quiet strength, or a playful animal brimming with joy? Understanding its natural behaviors can offer insights into the qualities it embodies.

Delve deeper by researching the symbolism associated with that particular species across different cultures. A fox, for instance, might symbolize cunning and adaptability, while a wise owl is often linked to knowledge and discernment. Look for parallels between the animal's symbolic nature and your own life path. Are you facing a situation that requires resourcefulness like the fox, or perhaps you're seeking guidance and wisdom like the owl?

The call of the wild isn't just about actively seeking out an animal encounter. It's about creating a space for synchronicity to occur. By being present in nature, with a curious and open mind, you allow the possibility of a meaningful connection with your spirit animal to unfold organically. The animal that appears most frequently, or the one that resonates most deeply with your intuition, might just hold the key to unlocking a deeper understanding of yourself and the path ahead.

Unexpected animal encounters in your daily life can also be powerful signs pointing towards your spirit animal. While venturing into nature allows for a more dedicated search, the spirit world can sometimes weave messages into the fabric of your everyday experiences. These seemingly random interactions deserve attention, for they might hold hidden significance and offer valuable clues about your spirit guide.

Consider the curious bird that taps persistently on your window. In some cultures, birds are seen as messengers from the spirit realm. The specific bird species can offer additional insights. A brightly colored hummingbird, known for its frenetic energy, might symbolize a need to embrace life's vibrancy. On the other hand, a wise old owl perched outside your window could be urging you to seek knowledge and hidden truths.

Even seemingly mundane interactions can hold meaning. A stray cat that seeks your attention could represent the need for independence and self-reliance, qualities often associated with felines. Perhaps you're in a phase of your life where establishing boundaries and trusting your intuition is paramount. Similarly, a majestic deer that pauses and gazes at you during your morning commute could be a reminder to slow down, appreciate the beauty around you, and find moments of peace amidst the daily rush.

The key lies in interpreting these encounters with an open mind and a touch of intuition. Consider the context of the interaction, the specific animal involved, and how its symbolic nature aligns with your current life experiences. Are you facing a challenge that requires the hawk's keen vision and focus? Or perhaps the rabbit's resourcefulness and adaptability would be a valuable asset in your current situation.

By acknowledging these unexpected encounters and seeking their deeper meaning, you open yourself to the possibility of deciphering the messages the spirit world might be sending you. The animal that appears most frequently, or the one that evokes the strongest emotional response, could very well be your spirit animal, offering guidance and support on your life's journey.

Delving into your creative side can be a powerful tool for connecting with your spirit animal. Unlike the more passive approaches of observation or meditation, creative exploration allows you to tap into your subconscious and intuition, bringing forth the essence of your spirit guide through artistic expression.

Journaling can be a useful tool in your quest to connect with your spirit animal. It provides a safe and quiet space to delve into your inner world, a place where intuition and subconscious whispers can be heard more clearly. Begin by setting a specific intention – to connect with your spirit animal. Let this intention guide your writing and open yourself to the possibility of receiving messages.

Within the pages of your journal, record any recurring dreams, visions, or animal encounters that have left a lasting impression. These seemingly random experiences might hold the key to unlocking the identity of your spirit guide. Pay close attention to any emotions that surfaced during these encounters. Did you feel a sense of awe or respect? Perhaps a surge of fear or curiosity? These emotional responses can offer valuable clues about the energy associated with your spirit animal.

Don't be afraid to delve deeper into the symbolism that arises. Jot down any mythological associations, cultural meanings, or personal connections you have with the animals that keep appearing. As you free-write, allow your thoughts to flow freely without judgment. Don't force any specific outcome – simply allow yourself to explore these themes and see where your intuition takes you. You might find yourself describing specific animal characteristics, the way it moves or interacts with its environment. These details could be whispers from your spirit animal, revealing its unique nature and the lessons it has to offer.

Through consistent journaling, patterns may begin to emerge. You might find yourself repeatedly drawn to a particular animal, its image appearing on the page alongside your anxieties, aspirations, or turning points in your life. This could be a sign that your spirit animal is trying to communicate with you. By keeping a dedicated record of your experiences and inner musings, your journal becomes a valuable roadmap on your journey of discovery, ultimately leading you closer to understanding and connecting with your spirit animal.

The artistic realm offers another powerful avenue for connecting with your spirit animal. Unlike a traditional portrait where you strive for a realistic image, here the goal is to tap into your intuition and allow it to guide your hand. Instead of forcing a specific image, take a deep breath and let your hand move freely across the page. Focus on the creative flow, the colors, shapes, and textures that emerge organically. Don't be surprised if, amidst the swirls and lines, an animal form begins to take shape. This could be the first glimpse of your spirit animal, emerging from your subconscious and revealing itself on the canvas.

The key lies in approaching this process with an open mind and a sense of trust. Trust that your intuition will guide you, that the colors you're drawn to and the shapes that flow from your hand hold deeper significance. Recurring symbols associated with specific animals might also appear in your artwork. Perhaps a powerful owl takes flight across your canvas, its wise eyes gazing out, or a majestic stag emerges from a forest of vibrant greens. These symbolic representations could be messages from your spirit animal, offering clues about its nature and the lessons it carries.

The power of artistic exploration doesn't stop at drawing and painting. Engaging in sculpting with clay or creating collages can be equally fruitful endeavors for connecting with your spirit animal. The use of different textures and materials allows you to express this connection on a more multi-sensory level. Imagine molding the fierce strength of a bear in clay, feeling the rough texture evoke its power and resilience. Or perhaps creating a collage using feathers, fur scraps, and natural elements becomes a way to honor the wildness and freedom associated with your spirit animal.

By letting go of preconceived notions and embracing the creative flow, you might be surprised by the animal forms that emerge and the messages they convey. This artistic journey isn't just about creating a masterpiece, but about opening a dialogue with your inner world and the spirit animal that resides there. So grab your paints, sculpt some clay, or let your imagination run wild with collage materials – you never know what powerful insights and connections await you on this creative path.

The true beauty of creative exploration in connecting with your spirit animal lies in its ability to bypass the limitations of the conscious mind. Unlike intellectual analysis, artistic expression allows you to tap into a deeper wellspring of knowing. As you lose yourself in the creative process, the chatter of the everyday mind fades away. This quieting allows for a more subtle, intuitive connection to emerge. In this space free from judgment and self-criticism, your spirit animal has the opportunity to reveal itself through symbolic imagery and intuitive expression.

The resulting artwork, whether it's a detailed drawing of a majestic wolf or an abstract collage filled with swirling colors and animal textures, becomes a bridge between your conscious mind and your subconscious. While you might not receive a clear, literal image of your spirit animal, the essence of its energy can be captured in the creative output. Perhaps a recurring symbol of feathers appears in your artwork, hinting at the freedom and adaptability associated with a hawk spirit guide. Or maybe the fierce energy of a bear manifests in bold strokes and powerful brushwork.

The key is to approach your artwork not just as an aesthetic creation, but as a window into your inner world. By quieting your analytical mind and allowing your intuition to take the lead, you create a space for your spirit animal to communicate with you through the language of symbols, colors, and textures. Once the artwork is complete, take some time to reflect on it. What emotions does it evoke? Are there recurring shapes or symbols that stand out to you? Research the symbolism associated with these elements and see if they resonate with any known animal characteristics.

Remember, the creative process is not about achieving artistic perfection. It's about creating a safe space for exploration and connection. The resulting artwork, in all its messy glory or unexpected beauty, becomes a powerful reminder of your connection with your spirit guide and the qualities it embodies. So don't be afraid to experiment, embrace the unknown, and trust that the creative flow will lead you closer to understanding your unique relationship with your spirit animal.

Guided Meditation

Guided meditations offer a powerful tool for those seeking to connect with their spirit animal, particularly for those who may not be able to embark on a traditional vision quest. Unlike vision quests, which often involve venturing into the wilderness and facing physical challenges, guided meditations provide a safe and accessible way to embark on this inward journey.

There are several ways to experience a guided meditation for connecting with your spirit animal. You can choose a self-guided meditation, following a recording or script designed to lead you through the process. For a more personalized experience, you can seek guidance from a spiritual leader or shaman familiar with spirit animal traditions. They can tailor the meditation to your specific needs and offer additional insights based on their knowledge and experience.

The ideal environment for your guided meditation should be peaceful and free from distractions. Dim the lights, put your phone on silent, and create a space that feels calming and inviting. You can use soothing music, essential oils, or gentle incense to further enhance the atmosphere. Most importantly, approach the meditation with an open mind and a receptive state. Release any expectations about what your spirit animal might look like or how you will encounter it. Simply allow yourself to be present in the moment and trust that the process will unfold organically.

During the meditation, the guide (whether a recording or a live person) will likely use visualization techniques to create a mental landscape conducive to encountering your spirit animal. You might find yourself walking through a lush forest teeming with life, exploring a vast meadow bathed in golden sunlight, or perhaps journeying to a place of personal significance, like a childhood treehouse or a favorite camping spot. While the specific location may vary, the key is the feeling it evokes within you – a sense of openness, peace, and connection to nature.

Throughout the guided meditation, the facilitator will use prompts to stimulate your imagination and deepen your connection to the natural world. They might ask you to pay close attention to the sounds you hear, the sensations in your body, or any specific animals that draw your attention. These prompts act as bridges, helping you navigate from the analytical mind to the realm of intuition, where a connection with your spirit animal might be found. By following the prompts, quieting your inner chatter, and allowing yourself to fully immerse in the experience, you open yourself to the possibility of encountering your spirit guide and receiving the messages it has to offer.

Immersing yourself completely in nature can also be a truly transformative way to experience a guided meditation for connecting with your spirit animal. Instead of a quiet space indoors, seek out a location in nature that resonates with you. This could be a serene forest clearing bathed in dappled sunlight, a secluded meadow teeming with wildflowers, or a rocky beach whispering secrets from the ocean. The key is to find a place that feels peaceful and allows you to fully connect with the surrounding environment.

Once you've found your natural sanctuary, take a few moments to ground yourself. Feel the earth beneath your bare feet (if comfortable) or the coolness of the grass against your skin. Notice the gentle breeze carrying the scent of pine needles or the salty tang of the ocean air. Let the sounds of rustling leaves, chirping birds, or crashing waves wash over you. This simple act of connecting with the elements allows you to become part of the natural world, fostering a deeper openness to encountering your spirit animal.

As you begin the guided meditation, visualize yourself entering this natural environment. Rather than imagining the landscape, focus on the sights, sounds, and sensations you're experiencing in real-time. Feel the warmth of the sun on your skin or the coolness of the shade beneath a towering tree. Notice the specific animals that inhabit this space. Are there playful squirrels scampering in the branches, or a majestic hawk soaring overhead? Observe them without judgment, simply allowing them to exist within your meditative space.

Should an animal capture your attention, don't force an interaction. Instead, observe its behavior and how it interacts with its surroundings. Does it radiate a sense of calm wisdom like an owl, or perhaps the playful energy of a young deer? Notice any emotions or intuitive feelings that arise as you connect with this animal.

The most important aspect of this nature meditation is to be fully present in the moment. While encountering a specific spirit animal might be a powerful experience, simply being open to the possibility within the embrace of nature is a gift in itself. The sights, sounds, and sensations of the natural world can offer valuable insights and a renewed sense of connection to the larger web of life. Remember, there's no right or wrong way to experience this meditation. Approach it with an open mind, trust your intuition, and allow the magic of nature to guide you on your journey towards connecting with your spirit animal.

Here's an example of how you can do a self guided meditation to find your spirit animal:

Guided Meditation: Encountering Your Spirit Animal

Preparation:

- Find a quiet, comfortable place where you won't be disturbed. Dim the lights or light some candles for a calming ambiance. You can also play soft, nature-themed music if that helps you relax.
- Sit or lie down in a position that allows you to relax completely. Close your eyes and take a few deep breaths, inhaling slowly through your

nose and exhaling completely through your mouth. With each breath, release any tension you hold in your body and quiet your mind.

The Journey Begins (5 minutes):

Imagine yourself standing at the edge of a peaceful forest. Sunlight filters through the leaves, casting dappled light on the soft earth beneath your feet. The air is filled with the sweet scent of wildflowers and the gentle chirping of unseen birds. Take a moment to absorb the beauty and serenity of this place.

As you step into the forest, feel the soft earth beneath your bare feet. Notice the warmth of the sun on your skin and the cool touch of leaves brushing against your arms. Pay attention to the sounds around you – the rustling of leaves in the breeze, the distant call of a bird, the trickling of a hidden stream. Allow yourself to be fully present in this moment, immersed in the sights, sounds, and smells of the forest.

Deepening the Connection (5 minutes):

Continue walking deeper into the forest. The path may wind and turn, but trust that it will lead you where you need to go. As you walk, notice if any particular animal catches your eye. Perhaps a deer grazes in a sunlit clearing, or a hawk circles overhead on powerful wings. Don't force an encounter, but simply observe any animals that appear, paying attention to how they make you feel.

You might also encounter other elements in the forest –
a shimmering waterfall, a towering tree, a field of
wildflowers. Notice if any of these elements hold a
special significance for you. Perhaps they evoke a
sense of peace, power, or joy. Allow yourself to be
drawn to these elements and see if they offer any clues
about your spirit animal.

Meeting Your Spirit Guide (5 minutes):

As you continue your journey, you might find yourself
arriving at a special place within the forest. It could be
a hidden clearing bathed in sunlight, a peaceful
meadow beside a stream, or perhaps a place you've
dreamt of before. This is a place of power and
connection, a place where you might encounter your
spirit animal.

Take a moment to stand still and be present in this
space. Open yourself to the possibility of encountering
your spirit animal. It might appear in a physical form –
a majestic stag, a soaring eagle, a wise owl. Or
perhaps you'll sense its presence through a feeling, a
sound, or an image that appears in your mind. Trust
your intuition and allow the encounter to unfold
naturally.

Receiving Messages (5 minutes):

If your spirit animal appears in a physical form, observe
its behavior. How does it move? Does it make any
sounds? Does it offer you any gifts or symbols? Pay
attention to any emotions you feel in its presence – joy,
fear, respect, or anything else. These emotions and

interactions can offer clues about the lessons your spirit animal carries.

If you don't encounter a physical form, don't be discouraged. The message from your spirit animal could come through a feeling, a sound, a color, or a symbol that appears in your mind. Hold onto this experience and reflect on it after the meditation. Research the symbolism associated with the message you received to see if it resonates with your current life experiences or offers any guidance.

Returning from the Journey (5 minutes):

When you feel complete with your experience, gently begin to bring your awareness back to your physical body. Wiggle your fingers and toes, and take a few deep breaths. When you're ready, slowly open your eyes. Take a moment to journal about your experience, recording the sights, sounds, emotions, and any symbols or messages you received.

Remember: This is just a guide. The most important aspect is to be open and receptive to the experience. Trust your intuition and allow your spirit animal to communicate with you in its own unique way. The messages received during this meditation, or subsequent encounters with your spirit animal, can offer valuable guidance and support on your life's journey.

However, it's important to remember that encountering a spirit animal during a guided meditation is not guaranteed. Sometimes, the most valuable aspect of these practices is the sense of peace and clarity they bring. Even if you don't encounter a specific animal, the process of introspection and connection with nature can be deeply insightful and offer valuable guidance on your life path.

Dreams and Visions

Dreams and visions have the potential to act as gateways to encountering your spirit animal. These encounters can be subtle or striking, cryptic or direct, but they all hold the potential to reveal valuable messages about your inner self and life path.

Dreams and visions, while both powerful tools for self-discovery, differ in their essence and how they manifest. Dreams are the fantastical narratives our minds weave during sleep. They can be vivid and emotionally charged, filled with symbolism and metaphors, but rarely feel grounded in reality. We often have little control over the content of dreams, and they can be nonsensical or even frightening. Visions, on the other hand, occur while we're awake and in an altered state of consciousness. They can feel more real and immediate than dreams, like seeing things with your inner eye rather than your physical one. Visions can be spontaneous or induced through meditation or rituals.

In the context of encountering your spirit animal, both dreams and visions can play a role. Pay attention to recurring themes or symbols involving specific animals in your dreams. Does a particular creature keep appearing, even if the dream itself seems nonsensical? This repetition might be a message from your subconscious, nudging you towards your spirit animal. Consider the symbolism associated with the animal – its natural behaviors, strengths, and weaknesses. Does its symbolic essence resonate with something within you? For instance, if a wise owl keeps appearing in your dreams, it might be urging you to develop your own wisdom and discernment. Similarly, a recurring image of a soaring hawk could symbolize the need for greater focus and determination in pursuing your goals.

The emotional connection you feel when encountering an animal in your dreams is another significant clue. Do you experience a sense of comfort and familiarity, or perhaps a surge of power or even a tinge of fear? These emotional responses can offer valuable insights into the message your spirit animal might be conveying. For example, feeling a sense of peace and tranquility during a dream encounter with a majestic deer might suggest the importance of finding harmony and gentleness within yourself. Conversely, if you feel a jolt of fear when encountering a snake in a vision, it could represent a hidden fear or challenge that you need to confront in your waking life.

To solidify your understanding of these dream encounters, consider keeping a dream journal. Jot down the details of your dreams and visions as soon as you wake up, paying close attention to any interactions you have with animals. Over time, recurring themes and symbols might surface, offering a clearer picture of the animal that might be your spirit guide. Meditation can also be a powerful tool for deciphering these dream messages. Quiet your mind and focus on the recurring animal image. See if any intuitive thoughts or feelings arise about its significance.

Remember, the literal form of the animal in your dreams may not be the most important element. Look beyond the surface and explore the deeper meaning it represents in your life. Ultimately, the most important factor is your own inner knowing. If a particular animal resonates with you on a deep level, if it evokes powerful emotions or a sense of familiarity, then it might very well be your spirit guide. The connection with your spirit animal is a lifelong exploration. As you grow and evolve, your understanding of its message and the wisdom it offers may deepen and transform over time. Trust your intuition, embrace the journey of discovery, and allow the dreams and visions to guide you towards a deeper understanding of yourself and the spirit animal that walks beside you.

Visions, those waking glimpses into a world beyond the physical, can be another powerful tool for encountering your spirit animal. Unlike dreams, which occur during sleep, visions happen when you're conscious but in an altered state of awareness. This heightened state allows for a deeper connection to your intuition and the symbolic language of the spirit world.

There's no single guaranteed method to induce a vision of your spirit animal, but certain practices can create fertile ground for this encounter. Meditation serves as a powerful tool for quieting the external chatter of the mind and opening yourself to receive messages from within. Focus on your breath, letting go of distracting thoughts and anxieties. As your mind becomes still, hold the intention of connecting with your spirit animal. Visualize yourself in a peaceful natural setting, open and receptive to any messages that may arise.

Sensory deprivation can also be a catalyst for visions. Find a quiet, dark space where you won't be interrupted. Lie down comfortably, close your eyes, and focus on relaxing your body. Cover your eyes with an eye mask to further eliminate external stimuli. Pay attention to any sounds, sensations, or images that emerge behind your closed eyelids. These could be the first stirrings of a vision, a symbolic representation of your spirit animal waiting to be deciphered.

Visions, because of their more conscious nature, can offer clearer messages. You might experience a waking vision of a specific animal, perhaps imbued with a sense of power or wisdom. The animal might even interact with you, offering guidance or protection. The emotional response you experience during these visions is also significant. Do you feel a sense of peace and knowing, or perhaps a challenge or a call to action? These emotions can provide clues about the message your spirit animal is trying to convey.

Ultimately, visions often arrive unexpectedly, like whispers on the wind. The key is to cultivate a state of openness and receptivity. Keep a dream journal handy, even for recording these waking visions. Jot down the details – the animal you saw, the emotions you felt, any symbols or messages that emerged. Reflect on these experiences, share them with a trusted friend or guide if you feel comfortable, and allow the pieces to come together organically. The vision of your spirit animal may not be a grand, Hollywood-style spectacle. It could be a fleeting image, a powerful feeling, or a subtle knowing that emerges over time. Trust the process, and remember, the journey of encountering your spirit animal is as important as the destination itself.

Spirit Walk or Vision Quest

In some indigenous cultures, the most profound way to connect with your spirit animal is through a traditional practice known as a spirit walk or vision quest. This is far more than a simple walk in the woods; it's a challenging and introspective journey designed to push you to your limits and open yourself to the spirit world. It's a solitary ritual undertaken by those seeking guidance, self-discovery, and the potential encounter with their spirit guide.

These vision quests are not for the faint of heart. They often involve fasting, spending extended periods of time alone in the wilderness, and sometimes even undergoing periods of sensory deprivation. The participant is stripped down to the bare essentials, forced to confront their inner demons and rely solely on their own strength and intuition. This harsh environment serves a purpose – to break down the barriers of the ego and create a space for deeper connection with the spirit world.

Traditionally, vision quests were seen as a rite of passage, particularly for young people on the cusp of adulthood. It was a test of courage, resilience, and their ability to connect with the unseen forces that govern life. By removing themselves from the comforts and distractions of daily life, participants enter a liminal space – a threshold between the physical world they know and the realm of spirits, dreams, and profound self-discovery. In this liminal space, stripped bare of external stimuli, the individual becomes more receptive to messages from the spirit world. It's in this state of heightened awareness that encounters with spirit animals are most likely to occur. These encounters can come in the form of dreams, visions, or even physical manifestations in the natural world. The messages and lessons received during a vision quest can be life-changing, offering guidance, strength, and a deeper understanding of one's place in the universe.

The spirit animal encountered during a vision quest is believed to be far more than just a random encounter. It's seen as a personal guide and protector, chosen specifically for the individual on their unique journey. This animal embodies qualities that resonate deeply with the individual's needs and aspirations at that particular point in their life. Imagine a young warrior embarking on a vision quest, yearning for strength and courage. They might encounter a powerful bear spirit, reflecting the inner strength and resilience needed to face future challenges. Or perhaps an aspiring artist, seeking inspiration and creativity, might encounter a vibrantly colored butterfly, symbolizing the transformative power of artistic expression. The spirit animal becomes a totem, a powerful symbol that offers not only guidance but also a sense of belonging and connection to something larger than oneself.

It's important to understand that the spirit walk or vision quest is not simply a way to "find" a spirit animal in the same way you might find a lost sock. It's a transformative experience, a crucible that pushes you to your limits and forces you to confront your inner self. Through the challenges of fasting, solitude, and potential sensory deprivation, participants develop a profound sense of self-reliance and a deeper connection with the natural world. They enter a liminal space, a threshold between the physical and the spiritual, where the walls between consciousness and subconscious begin to thin. In this state of heightened awareness, the individual becomes more receptive to messages from the spirit world, and an encounter with a spirit animal becomes a possibility.

However, even if a physical encounter doesn't occur, the vision quest itself holds immense value. The lessons learned, the struggles overcome, and the insights gleaned from this experience all contribute to the individual's personal growth. The spirit animal encountered, if any, becomes a symbol of this profound transformation. It represents the courage it took to embark on the journey, the resilience displayed in the face of hardship, and the wisdom gained from connecting with the deeper aspects of oneself. Whether a majestic eagle soaring through the sky or a wise old owl perched on a branch, the spirit animal serves as a reminder of the transformative power of the vision quest and the potential for growth that resides within each of us.

The traditions surrounding vision quests, also known as spirit walks, vary depending on the culture and lineage. However, some core elements bind these practices together.

Traditionally, vision quests, also known as spirit walks, were solitary journeys undertaken by individuals seeking profound personal growth, guidance on a critical life decision, or a rite of passage marking a transition into a new phase of life. These individuals ventured into the wilderness alone, often for several days or even weeks, with minimal provisions. This deliberate act of stripping away the comforts and distractions of daily life served a specific purpose. By immersing themselves in the raw power and solitude of nature, they sought to heighten their inner awareness and enter a state of heightened receptivity. In the quietude of the wilderness, stripped bare of external stimuli, the individual embarked on a deep introspective journey, confronting their inner demons, and unearthing hidden truths.

However, the solitary vision quest, while a powerful tradition, isn't for everyone. Recognizing this, contemporary settings have seen a rise in guided vision quests led by experienced facilitators. These facilitators, often shamans or spiritual guides, possess deep knowledge of the traditions and practices associated with vision quests. Their role extends beyond simply leading participants to a secluded location. They offer invaluable support and guidance throughout the experience. This can include helping participants set clear intentions for their quest, providing practical advice on wilderness survival skills, and ensuring the safety and well-being of participants during their time in nature. In some cases, these facilitators may even have undergone vision quests themselves and can offer insights and wisdom gleaned from their own experiences. The presence of a trusted guide can provide a sense of security and allow participants to fully immerse themselves in the transformative potential of the vision quest.

Regardless of whether you choose to embark on a solitary vision quest or participate in a guided one, some level of preparation is essential to ensure a safe and successful experience. Physical fitness is a key element, particularly if your quest takes you into a remote wilderness area. Before setting out, consider gradually building your endurance through regular walks or hikes that progressively increase in difficulty. This will help you navigate the potential challenges of uneven terrain, long distances, and carrying essential supplies.

Equipping yourself with basic survival skills is another crucial safety measure. Depending on the location of your vision quest, this might involve learning how to build a fire for warmth and cooking, identifying edible plants and safe water sources, and understanding basic first-aid principles. There are numerous resources available online and in libraries that offer wilderness survival training and guidance. Even if you're participating in a guided quest, possessing these skills can provide a sense of self-reliance and confidence during your time in nature.

Finally, ensuring you have the proper clothing and gear for the environment is vital. Research the typical weather conditions for the time of year and location of your vision quest. Pack sturdy footwear suitable for uneven terrain, weather-appropriate clothing that provides warmth or protection from the elements, and a basic first-aid kit. A headlamp or flashlight, a map and compass (and the knowledge of how to use them), and a communication device like a personal locator beacon (PLB) can be valuable safety measures, especially on a solitary quest. By taking these steps to prepare your body and gather the necessary supplies, you can approach your vision quest with a sense of confidence and focus your energy on the introspective journey that lies ahead.

While physical preparation is crucial for a vision quest, equally important is preparing your mind and spirit for the profound experience that awaits. This inner preparation lays the foundation for a focused and open mindset, allowing you to fully engage with the transformative potential of the quest.

Meditation serves as a powerful tool for quieting the external noise and chatter of the mind. Regular meditation practice leading up to your vision quest can help you cultivate a sense of inner calm and focus. By quieting your thoughts and anxieties, you create a space within yourself to receive the messages and insights that may arise during your time in nature.

Spending time in nature in quiet contemplation is another way to prepare your spirit for the vision quest. Immersing yourself in the sights, sounds, and smells of the natural world can help you reconnect with your intuition and inner wisdom. Pay attention to the subtle messages that nature offers – the rustling of leaves, the songs of birds, the flow of a stream. These elements can act as gateways to a deeper understanding of yourself and the world around you.

The very core of your vision quest lies in setting a clear intention, a guiding light that illuminates your path during this transformative experience. While introspection and self-discovery are inherent benefits, on this quest, your primary focus is to encounter your spirit animal. Are you yearning for a deeper connection with this powerful guide who will walk beside you through life's journey? Do you long to understand the unique qualities and wisdom your spirit animal embodies? Defining this intention as your focal point increases the likelihood of receiving meaningful encounters or insights that will lead you to unlock the identity of your spirit animal. By setting this clear purpose, you open yourself to a deeper level of communication with the natural world and the spirit realm, ultimately paving the way for a profound connection with your spirit guide.

Through meditation, connecting with nature, and setting a clear intention, you prime your mind and spirit for the transformative potential of the vision quest. With a focused and open mindset, you'll be better equipped to navigate the internal landscapes you encounter during your time in solitude, ultimately emerging from the experience with a renewed sense of self-awareness and a deeper connection to the world around you.

The location of a vision quest, particularly one undertaken in search of your spirit animal, holds a significant symbolic weight. Ideally, it should be a place steeped in nature, far from the distractions and noise of daily life. This could be a remote wilderness area, untouched by human development, where the raw power of nature reigns supreme. Imagine yourself venturing deep into a dense forest, sunlight filtering through the canopy, the earthy scent of damp soil filling your senses. Alternatively, a mountaintop with breathtaking vistas could be your chosen location. Standing at a high elevation, surrounded by the vastness of the sky and the rolling hills below, fosters a sense of humility and connection to something larger than yourself. Even a secluded spot within a local park can suffice, as long as it provides a haven of quietude where you can commune with your inner world.

The duration of your vision quest can vary widely, depending on your personal preferences and intentions. A single night spent under the starry sky, immersed in nature's nightly chorus, can be a powerful experience. However, some individuals seek a more extended period of isolation, embarking on quests that last for several days or even weeks. This extended solitude allows them to delve deeper into their subconscious, stripping away the layers of daily life and creating space for their spirit animal to reveal itself.

Fasting is a common element incorporated into many vision quests, especially those in search of a spirit animal. By abstaining from food, you symbolically let go of the physical world and its needs. This act of self-denial is believed to heighten your senses and awareness, making you more receptive to the subtle messages and encounters that might lead you to your spirit animal. It's important to approach fasting with caution, however. Safety is paramount. Always consult with a healthcare professional before undertaking a prolonged fast, especially if you have any underlying health conditions. Listen to your body – if you experience excessive fatigue, dizziness, or any other concerning symptoms, break the fast and prioritize your well-being. Remember, the goal of the vision quest is to foster growth, not endanger your health.

An encounter with your spirit animal on a vision quest can unfold in a fascinating and unpredictable way. For some fortunate individuals, it might happen right at the outset. A vivid dream filled with symbolism or a powerful interaction with a physical animal shortly after entering the wilderness could be the first sign. This immediate encounter serves as a potent introduction to the energy and wisdom your spirit animal embodies.

More commonly, the discovery of your spirit animal is a gradual process that unfolds throughout the vision quest. As you delve deeper into solitude and introspection, pay close attention to recurring symbols, dreams, or visions that feature specific animals. These encounters may not be clear at first, but as the quest progresses, they may become more vivid and impactful. Perhaps a particular bird species keeps appearing in your dreams, or you find yourself drawn to the tracks of a certain animal during your daily walks in nature. These repetitive experiences hold significance and can offer clues about the identity of your spirit animal.

The true magic of the vision quest, however, sometimes reveals itself only after you return to daily life. Journaling about your experiences and reflecting on them with friends and family. Through this process of reflection and interpretation, the identity of your spirit animal may finally come into focus.

Remember, the vision quest isn't a competition to find your spirit animal as quickly as possible. It's a deeply personal journey of self-discovery. Approach it with an open mind and a willingness to learn and grow. The deeper you connect with nature and the more present you become in the moment, the more receptive you'll be to the subtle messages that might reveal your spirit animal. Trust the process. Even if you don't have a clear-cut encounter during the quest itself, the lessons learned and the heightened awareness you cultivate can pave the way for the identification of your spirit animal in the days, weeks, or even months that follow. The spirit world works in mysterious ways, and the revelation of your spirit guide may unfold in ways you least expect.

The culmination of your vision quest doesn't mark the end of the journey, but rather a new chapter. Upon returning, especially from a solitary quest, processing your experiences is vital to unlock the transformative power of the encounter with your spirit animal. Sharing your experiences with a trusted friend, family member, or spiritual guide can be an invaluable tool in this process.

Imagine yourself returning from your vision quest, brimming with vivid memories, powerful emotions, and perhaps even symbolic dreams or visions. These experiences can be complex and layered, requiring careful unpacking. A trusted friend or family member can offer a safe space for you to share your story without judgment. They can listen intently as you describe the sights, sounds, and encounters you experienced in nature. Their presence and support can help you ground yourself and begin to make sense of the fragmented pieces of your vision quest.

Perhaps the most valuable resource for processing your vision quest is a spiritual guide. These individuals often possess a deep understanding of the traditions and practices surrounding vision quests and spirit animals. They can help you interpret the symbolic language of your experiences and translate the messages from your spirit animal into practical applications for your daily life. By sharing your journey with a spiritual guide, you gain not only an interpreter, but also a mentor who can help you integrate the wisdom gleaned from your vision quest into your ongoing journey of self-discovery.

Whether you choose to confide in a friend, family member, or spiritual guide, the act of sharing your experiences is an essential part of integrating the lessons learned from your vision quest. Through open communication and reflection, you can unlock the transformative power of this profound experience and gain a deeper understanding of yourself, your connection to the natural world, and the spirit animal who now walks beside you.

Throughout your vision quest, remember that your body and mind are your primary instruments. Treat them with respect and listen closely to their signals. Pay close attention to your physical state. Are you experiencing excessive fatigue, dizziness, or dehydration? Is the environment harsher than you anticipated, demanding more exertion than you're prepared for? Don't be afraid to adjust your plans accordingly. There's no shame in shortening your quest or seeking shelter if your physical well-being is compromised. Remember, the goal is to create a safe and receptive space for encountering your spirit animal, not to push yourself to the point of exhaustion or injury.

Your mental state is equally important. The solitude and introspection inherent in a vision quest can be both exhilarating and challenging. Pay attention to your emotional well-being. Are feelings of anxiety or loneliness overwhelming you? Are you struggling to maintain focus or feeling overwhelmed by sensory input? If so, don't hesitate to adjust your course. Meditation techniques like deep breathing exercises can help manage anxiety and bring you back to a centered state. Taking short walks or engaging in mindful activities like journaling can help ground yourself and process the emotions arising during your quest. Ultimately, if you feel unsafe or overwhelmed, there's no shame in cutting your quest short. Returning to civilization and regrouping doesn't diminish the value of the experience. You can always revisit the vision quest in the future, perhaps better prepared or with a slightly different intention.

The beauty of a vision quest lies in its deeply personal nature. There's no single "correct" way to perform it. The most important aspect is to approach it with respect for the traditions and the power of nature. Set a clear intention for your quest, focusing on connecting with your spirit animal. Prepare yourself physically and mentally, but also embrace the element of flexibility. Listen to your body and mind, and trust your intuition. The most profound lessons and encounters may not always occur in the way you anticipate. By approaching the experience with respect, intention, and a willingness to learn and grow, you open yourself to the transformative potential of the vision quest and the guidance of your spirit animal. The journey itself, with all its challenges and triumphs, becomes a valuable part of the process, leading you to a deeper understanding of yourself and the world around you.

Your Spirit Animal and it's Meaning

Encountering your spirit animal is a transformative experience, a moment of self-discovery that goes beyond simply identifying a cool creature you resonate with. It's about understanding the qualities and energies this animal embodies and how that knowledge can empower you on your life path. Here's how you can leverage this connection:

Consider the natural strengths and characteristics associated with your spirit animal. Is it known for its unwavering wisdom like the owl, its fierce courage like the lion, or its remarkable adaptability like the fox? Reflect on how you can cultivate these strengths within yourself. Perhaps your spirit animal is the bear, renowned for its inner fortitude and resilience. During challenging times, you can tap into this energy to persevere or use it to chase your goals with unwavering determination.

Observe how your spirit animal navigates the world. Does it hunt with strategic precision like a hawk, form deep social bonds like the elephant, or possess a playful and inquisitive nature like the dolphin? Consider how these behaviors can inspire your own approach to life. Maybe your spirit animal, the wolf, embodies a powerful sense of loyalty and teamwork, encouraging you to nurture stronger connections with those you hold dear.

Be mindful of recurring symbols. Pay attention to how your spirit animal starts appearing in your daily life – in a book you're reading, a song that resonates with you, or even a fleeting encounter in nature. These can be seen as subtle signs or reminders from your spirit guide, nudging you in a particular direction. For instance, if your spirit animal is the butterfly, noticing butterflies frequently could symbolize a time of transformation or new beginnings on your horizon.

Many cultures believe spirit animals offer a form of "medicine" – their wisdom and energy meant to guide and heal. Think about the challenges you're currently facing. Can the qualities of your spirit animal offer guidance or support? If your spirit animal is the snake, known for shedding its skin, it could be a message to embrace change and let go of what no longer serves you.

The connection with your spirit animal is an ongoing dialogue. As you learn more about the animal and its symbolism, reflect on how it applies to your life experiences. Use this newfound awareness to navigate challenges, make decisions, and embrace your full potential. Remember, your spirit animal isn't a genie granting wishes, but rather a wise companion offering guidance and encouragement on your life's journey. Walk alongside your spirit animal, learn from its wisdom, and allow it to empower you to become the best version of yourself.

Let's delve into some of the fascinating creatures that frequently appear as spirit animals and explore the symbolism they carry.

Bear

The bear, a magnificent creature with a thick coat and imposing presence, frequently appears as a spirit animal. Its symbolism is rich and multifaceted, encompassing both positive and negative traits that can serve as valuable guides on our life paths.

Embracing Inner Strength and Power:

- **Strength and Confidence:** The bear embodies unwavering strength and unwavering confidence. It reminds us of our own inner fortitude, the power to overcome challenges and chase our dreams with unwavering determination.
- **Protective Power:** Like a mother bear fiercely protecting her cubs, the bear spirit animal signifies protective power, a reminder to stand up for ourselves and those we love.
- **Courage:** The bear doesn't shy away from challenges. It urges us to face our fears and step outside our comfort zones to embrace new opportunities.

Exploring the Emotional Landscape:

- **Nurturing and Caring:** Beyond physical strength, the bear spirit delves into the realm of emotions. It symbolizes the nurturing and protective nature of mothers, reminding us to extend compassion and care towards ourselves and others.

- **Healing and Protection:** This powerful spirit guide is also associated with healing and protection, offering solace and guidance during times of emotional turmoil.
- **Introspection and Self-Discovery:** The bear's comfort in solitude signifies the importance of introspection and self-discovery. It encourages us to carve out space for quiet reflection and connect with our inner wisdom.

Grounding and Connection:

- **Groundedness:** The grounded nature of the bear reminds us to stay connected to the earth and our primal instincts, finding stability and peace in the natural world.

The Shadow Side of the Bear:

However, the bear's symbolism isn't without its complexities. Just as a bear fiercely defends its territory, the shadow side of this spirit animal can manifest as:

- **Aggression and Possessiveness:** It can serve as a cautionary tale against letting anger or territoriality cloud our judgment.
- **Unreliable Relationships:** In relationships, an overabundance of bear energy might symbolize a tendency to be unreliable or emotionally overwhelming.

- **Resistance to Change:** The bear's natural power can also represent a resistance to change or a fear of stepping outside of established routines.

A Forceful Messenger:

Ultimately, the bear spirit animal is a powerful messenger, urging us to:

- **Confront Fears:** The bear challenges us to confront our fears and anxieties.
- **Test Boundaries:** It encourages us to push our boundaries and explore new possibilities.
- **Embrace Strength:** The bear reminds us to tap into our inner strength and channel it into courage and confidence.

By acknowledging both the positive and negative aspects of the bear's symbolism, we gain valuable insights into ourselves and the potential to live a more balanced and fulfilling life. As we walk alongside this powerful spirit guide, we learn valuable lessons about strength, introspection, and the importance of staying grounded.

Fox

The fox, a sly and resourceful creature with a keen eye and sharp wit, is a frequent visitor in the spirit world. Its symbolism is rich and multifaceted, embodying both positive and negative traits that can offer valuable guidance on your life path.

Embracing Cleverness and Resourcefulness:

- **Intelligence and Cunning:** The fox is renowned for its intelligence and cunning. It encourages you to develop your problem-solving skills, think creatively, and approach challenges with strategic thinking.
- **Adaptability:** Highly adaptable, the fox spirit animal reminds you to be flexible and adjust your approach as needed. Life is full of unexpected twists and turns, and the fox's energy helps you navigate them with grace.
- **Resourcefulness:** The fox thrives by making the most of its environment. This spirit guide encourages you to be resourceful, find creative solutions, and use your talents to your advantage.

Exploring the Realm of Perception:

- **Keen Observation:** The fox possesses exceptional eyesight and hearing, symbolizing the importance of keen observation and awareness of your surroundings. Pay attention to subtle details, and trust your intuition to guide you.

- **Illusion and Deception:** Be mindful of the fox's association with illusion and deception. This doesn't necessarily imply negativity, but rather a reminder to be discerning and not take everything at face value. Look beyond the surface and seek the truth.

Balancing Playfulness and Independence:

- **Playfulness and Joy:** The fox spirit animal injects a dose of playfulness and joy into your life. Don't be afraid to embrace your sense of humor and find moments of lightheartedness, even amidst challenges.
- **Independence and Self-Reliance:** The solitary nature of the fox signifies independence and self-reliance. You have the strength and resourcefulness to navigate life's journey on your own terms.

The Shadow Side of the Fox:

The fox's symbolism also carries some complexities:

- **Mischief and Manipulation:** While cleverness is a positive trait, the shadow side of the fox can manifest as mischief or manipulation. Be mindful of using your cunning for good, not personal gain.
- **Deception and Dishonesty:** The association with illusion can also represent a tendency towards deception or dishonesty. The fox spirit

animal reminds you to act with integrity and build trust in your relationships.

A Messenger of Opportunity:

Ultimately, the fox spirit animal is a messenger of opportunity. It encourages you to:

- **Embrace Your Intellect:** Develop your problem-solving skills and approach challenges with strategic thinking.
- **Adapt to Change:** Be flexible and adjust your approach as needed to navigate life's unexpected turns.
- **Seize Opportunities:** The fox spirit animal nudges you to be resourceful and seize opportunities that come your way.

As you walk alongside this cunning spirit guide, you learn to navigate life with intelligence, adaptability, and a touch of playfulness.

Turtle

The turtle, a creature of ancient lineage with a sturdy shell and a slow but steady pace, is a powerful symbol in the spirit world. Its symbolism is rich and multifaceted, offering guidance on patience, perseverance, and living a life of stability and purpose.

Embracing Patience and Perseverance:

- **Slow and Steady Wins the Race:** The turtle's measured pace reminds us that true progress often comes through consistent effort and unwavering patience. Don't get discouraged by setbacks; focus on moving forward, one step at a time.
- **Inner Strength and Determination:** Beneath the turtle's seemingly slow exterior lies immense inner strength and determination. It encourages you to tap into your own resilience and keep moving forward, even when the path gets challenging.

Finding Stability and Protection:

- **Groundedness and Security:** The turtle's strong shell symbolizes groundedness and security. It reminds you to connect with your core values and build a foundation for a stable and fulfilling life.
- **Protection and Retreat:** The ability to withdraw into its shell signifies the importance of

self-protection and taking time for solitude and introspection when needed.

Living a Life of Wisdom and Connection:

- **Ancient Wisdom:** The turtle, a creature that has walked the earth for millions of years, embodies ancient wisdom and the cyclical nature of life. It encourages you to learn from the past, embrace the present, and trust the natural flow of life.
- **Connection to the Earth:** Deeply connected to the earth element, the turtle spirit animal reminds you to nurture your connection with nature. Spend time outdoors, appreciate the beauty of the natural world, and find peace in its grounding energy.

The Shadow Side of the Turtle:

The turtle's symbolism also carries some complexities:

- **Fear of Change:** The turtle's preference for routine and stability can sometimes manifest as a fear of change or resistance to trying new things. The turtle spirit animal reminds you that growth often requires stepping outside your comfort zone.
- **Isolation and Withdrawal:** While solitude is important, an overabundance of turtle energy can lead to excessive isolation or withdrawal from social interaction.

A Gentle Guide on Your Journey:

Ultimately, the turtle spirit animal is a gentle guide, urging you to:

- **Embrace Patience:** Approach life's challenges with patience and perseverance. Slow and steady progress is more sustainable than a quick burst of energy.
- **Find Your Inner Strength:** Tap into your inner resilience and determination to overcome obstacles and achieve your goals.
- **Seek Stability and Grounding:** Build a solid foundation for your life based on your core values and principles.

By understanding the symbolism of the turtle, you gain valuable insights into your own approach to life. As you walk alongside this wise spirit guide, you learn the importance of patience, perseverance, and living a life of purpose and deep connection with the natural world.

Beaver

The beaver, an industrious architect of the natural world, with its impressive dams and tireless work ethic, frequently appears as a spirit animal. Its symbolism is rich and multifaceted, offering valuable lessons about hard work, resourcefulness, and the importance of creating a secure foundation for yourself and those you love.

Embracing Diligence and Resourcefulness:

- **Hard Work and Determination:** The beaver is a tireless worker, renowned for its ability to tackle large projects with dedication and perseverance. If the beaver is your spirit animal, it might be urging you to channel your own inner industriousness and see your projects through to completion.
- **Resourcefulness and Problem-Solving:** Beavers are resourceful creatures, adept at using their environment to their advantage. This spirit animal encourages you to be innovative and find creative solutions to challenges.

Building a Strong Foundation:

- **Planning and Strategy:** Beavers meticulously plan and construct their dams, symbolizing the importance of planning and strategy in achieving your goals. Take the time to envision your desired outcome and create a roadmap to get there.

- **Creating Security and Stability:** The sturdy dams built by beavers represent the creation of security and stability in your life. The beaver spirit animal reminds you to focus on building a strong foundation, whether it's in your career, relationships, or personal well-being.

Community and Collaboration:

- **Cooperation and Teamwork:** Beavers are social creatures who work together to achieve common goals. This spirit animal emphasizes the importance of collaboration and teamwork. Surround yourself with supportive people and leverage the power of working together.

The Shadow Side of the Beaver:

The beaver's symbolism also carries some complexities:

- **Workaholism and Overexertion:** The beaver's relentless work ethic can sometimes manifest as workaholism or a tendency to overexert yourself. Remember to prioritize rest and self-care to avoid burnout.
- **Controlling Tendencies:** The beaver's focus on building and control can, in its shadow aspect, represent controlling tendencies in relationships or a resistance to letting go.

A Messenger of Purposeful Action:

Ultimately, the beaver spirit animal is a messenger of purposeful action. It encourages you to:

- **Embrace Hard Work:** See challenges as opportunities to develop your skills and work ethic.
- **Be Resourceful:** Think creatively and find innovative solutions to overcome obstacles.
- **Build a Strong Foundation:** Invest time and energy in creating a secure and fulfilling life.
- **Collaborate with Others:** Embrace the power of teamwork and build strong relationships with supportive people.

By understanding the symbolism of the beaver, you gain valuable insights into your approach to work, relationships, and goal setting. As you walk alongside this industrious spirit guide, you learn the importance of perseverance, resourcefulness, and creating a life of purpose and stability.

Eagle

Soaring through the vastness of the sky, the eagle is a powerful and revered symbol in many cultures. As a spirit animal, the eagle carries immense symbolism, offering guidance on leadership, vision, freedom, and spiritual connection.

Embracing Leadership and Power:

- **Strength and Authority:** The eagle's majestic presence embodies strength, authority, and leadership qualities. If the eagle is your spirit animal, it might be urging you to step into your own power and take charge of your life.
- **Vision and Focus:** With its keen eyesight, the eagle soars high above, able to see the bigger picture. This spirit animal encourages you to develop a clear vision for your goals and maintain focus as you pursue them.

Seeking Freedom and Independence:

- **Unbounded Spirit:** The eagle's ability to soar freely represents a yearning for independence and freedom. It might be a nudge to break free from limitations, both self-imposed and external, and embrace your authentic self.
- **Breaking Through Challenges:** The eagle effortlessly navigates strong winds and high altitudes, symbolizing the ability to overcome challenges and rise above obstacles.

Connecting with the Spiritual Realm:

- **Spiritual Connection:** Many cultures view the eagle as a bridge between the physical and spiritual realms. This spirit animal encourages you to cultivate your intuition and connect with your higher purpose.
- **Renewal and Transformation:** The eagle's ability to shed its feathers and renew itself signifies transformation and the potential for personal growth.

The Shadow Side of the Eagle:

The eagle's symbolism also carries some complexities:

- **Arrogance and Domination:** The eagle's powerful nature can sometimes manifest as arrogance, dominance, or a tendency to control others. The eagle spirit animal reminds you to use your power with wisdom and compassion.
- **Ruthlessness and Aggression:** The eagle's predatory instincts can represent a shadow aspect of ruthlessness or aggression. Be mindful of using your power ethically and with respect for others.

A Messenger of Inspiration:

Ultimately, the eagle spirit animal is a messenger of inspiration. It encourages you to:

- **Embrace Your Leadership Potential:** Develop your leadership skills and use your power to inspire and motivate others.
- **Maintain a Clear Vision:** Set ambitious goals, cultivate a clear vision, and stay focused on achieving them.
- **Seek Freedom and Independence:** Break free from limitations and embrace your authentic self.
- **Nurture Your Spiritual Connection:** Develop your intuition and explore your connection to the spiritual realm.

By understanding the symbolism of the eagle, you gain valuable insights into your strengths and potential areas for growth. As you walk alongside this majestic spirit guide, you learn to soar high, embrace challenges, and lead a life of purpose and inspiration.

Otter

The otter, a playful and social creature often seen frolicking in rivers and streams, holds a special place as a spirit animal. Its symbolism is rich and multifaceted, offering valuable lessons about joy, adaptability, community, and navigating life's currents with grace.

Embracing Playfulness and Positivity:

- **Joy and Enthusiasm:** The otter's playful nature embodies joy, enthusiasm, and a zest for life. If the otter is your spirit animal, it might be a reminder to find moments of lightheartedness and laughter even amidst challenges.
- **Positive Outlook:** Otters tend to approach life with optimism and a sense of wonder. This spirit animal encourages you to cultivate a positive outlook and find joy in the simple things.

Adaptability and Resourcefulness:

- **Thriving in Change:** Otters are highly adaptable creatures, comfortable in both water and on land. This spirit animal reminds you to be flexible and adjust your approach as needed to navigate life's ever-changing currents.
- **Resourcefulness and Problem-Solving:** Otters are resourceful creatures, adept at using tools and their environment to their advantage. The otter spirit animal nudges you to be creative

and find innovative solutions to overcome obstacles.

Community and Collaboration:

- **Social Connection and Teamwork:** Otters are highly social creatures, living and working together in playful groups. This spirit animal emphasizes the importance of fostering strong relationships and collaborating with others.
- **Communication and Cooperation:** Effective communication and teamwork are essential for otters to thrive. The otter spirit animal reminds you to hone your communication skills and work cooperatively towards shared goals.

The Shadow Side of the Otter:

The otter's symbolism also carries some complexities:

- **Scattered Energy and Lack of Focus:** The otter's playful and social nature can sometimes manifest as scattered energy or a lack of focus. The otter spirit animal reminds you to balance playfulness with responsibility and prioritize tasks when needed.
- **Naivety and Inattention to Danger:** The otter's carefree attitude can sometimes lead to naivety or a disregard for potential dangers. This spirit animal encourages you to maintain a healthy balance between optimism and caution.

A Messenger of Flow and Connection:

Ultimately, the otter spirit animal is a messenger of flow and connection. It encourages you to:

- **Embrace Playfulness:** Find joy in the simple things and cultivate a sense of wonder in your everyday life.
- **Adapt to Change:** Be flexible and resourceful in navigating life's unexpected turns.
- **Nurture Relationships:** Build strong connections with loved ones and collaborate effectively with others.
- **Go with the Flow:** Approach life with a sense of optimism and trust that the current will carry you in the right direction.

By understanding the symbolism of the otter, you gain valuable insights into your approach to life, relationships, and challenges. As you walk alongside this playful spirit guide, you learn to navigate life's currents with grace, resourcefulness, and a sense of joy.

Wolf

The wolf, a majestic creature often shrouded in myth and legend, frequently appears as a powerful spirit animal. Its symbolism is rich and multifaceted, encompassing both positive and negative traits that can serve as valuable guides on your life path.

Embracing Strength and Loyalty:

- **Inner Strength and Confidence:** The wolf embodies unwavering inner strength and unwavering confidence. It reminds you of your own resilience and the power to overcome challenges with courage and determination.
- **Fierce Loyalty and Protection:** Wolves are fiercely loyal to their pack, protecting their kin with unwavering devotion. The wolf spirit animal signifies the importance of loyalty and commitment in your relationships, encouraging you to stand by those you love.

Harnessing Independence and Freedom:

- **Independent Spirit:** The wolf's solitary nature symbolizes independence and self-reliance. You have the strength and resourcefulness to navigate life's journey on your own terms.
- **Freedom and Exploration:** The wolf's howl echoes through vast territories, representing a yearning for freedom and exploration. The wolf

spirit animal might be urging you to break free from limitations and explore new horizons.

Community and Communication:

- **Strength in Numbers:** While independent, wolves also form strong social bonds within their packs. This spirit animal emphasizes the importance of community and collaboration. Surround yourself with supportive people who uplift and inspire you.
- **Effective Communication:** Wolves communicate through a complex system of vocalizations and body language. The wolf spirit animal reminds you to hone your communication skills and express yourself clearly.

The Shadow Side of the Wolf:

The wolf's symbolism also carries some complexities:

- **Dominance and Control:** The hierarchical structure of wolf packs can manifest as a shadow aspect of dominance or a controlling nature. The wolf spirit animal reminds you to use your strength with compassion and avoid manipulating others.
- **Fear and Mistrust:** Wolves are naturally cautious creatures, and their shadow side can represent fear or a reluctance to trust others. The wolf spirit animal encourages you to confront your fears and cultivate healthy relationships built on trust.

A Messenger of Intuition and Teamwork:

Ultimately, the wolf spirit animal is a messenger of intuition and teamwork. It encourages you to:

- **Tap into Your Inner Strength:** Embrace your inner resilience and use it to overcome challenges with courage and confidence.
- **Cultivate Loyalty:** Nurture strong and loyal relationships with those who matter most.
- **Embrace Independence:** Carve your own path and explore new possibilities.
- **Seek Supportive Connections:** Build a strong support system and collaborate effectively with others.
- **Trust Your Intuition:** Honor your gut feelings and develop your intuition as a valuable guide.

As you walk alongside this powerful spirit guide, you learn the importance of courage, loyalty, independence, and navigating life's journey with both independence and a sense of belonging.

Panther

The panther, a sleek and enigmatic creature shrouded in mystery, holds a captivating presence as a spirit animal. Its symbolism is rich and multifaceted, encompassing power, grace, protection, and the ability to navigate unseen realms.

Embracing Power and Grace:

- **Inner Strength and Confidence:** The panther embodies a quiet yet potent inner strength. It reminds you of your own hidden power and the ability to achieve your goals with grace and determination.
- **Effortless Movement and Adaptability:** The panther's ability to move silently and with incredible agility signifies adaptability and resourcefulness. You have the potential to navigate complex situations with fluidity and overcome challenges with elegance.

Protection and Intuition:

- **Fierce Protector:** Panthers are known for their fierce protectiveness of their territory and young. The panther spirit animal can represent a guardian spirit, offering a sense of security and protection to you and your loved ones.
- **Intuition and Hidden Knowledge:** The panther's association with darkness and the unseen realm signifies a connection to intuition

and hidden knowledge. This spirit animal encourages you to trust your gut feelings and tap into your inner wisdom.

The Shadow Side of the Panther:

The panther's symbolism also carries some complexities:

- **Deception and Secrecy:** The panther's ability to move unseen can sometimes manifest as a shadow aspect of deception or secrecy. The panther spirit animal reminds you to act with integrity and avoid manipulating others.
- **Fear of the Unknown:** The panther's connection to darkness can represent a fear of the unknown or a reluctance to step outside your comfort zone. The panther spirit animal encourages you to embrace new experiences and confront your fears with courage.

A Messenger of Hidden Potential:

Ultimately, the panther spirit animal is a messenger of hidden potential. It encourages you to:

- **Embrace Your Inner Strength:** Develop your inner power and confidence, trusting your ability to achieve your goals.
- **Move with Grace and Adaptability:** Navigate life's challenges with resourcefulness and find solutions with finesse.
- **Protect What Matters Most:** Fiercely protect your loved ones and the values you hold dear.

- **Trust Your Intuition:** Develop your intuition and use it as a valuable guide in life's decisions.
- **Embrace New Experiences:** Step outside your comfort zone and explore the unknown with courage and curiosity.

By understanding the symbolism of the panther, you gain valuable insights into your strengths and areas for growth. As you walk alongside this powerful spirit guide, you learn to harness your inner power, navigate unseen realms with intuition, and embrace life's mysteries with grace and courage.

Dolphin

The dolphin, a social and intelligent creature known for its playful spirit and dazzling acrobatics, is a cherished symbol in many cultures and frequently appears as a spirit animal. Its symbolism is rich and multifaceted, offering guidance on communication, joy, emotional intelligence, and navigating life's currents with ease.

Embracing Playfulness and Joy:

- **Finding Joy and Harmony:** The dolphin's playful nature embodies the importance of finding joy and lightness in life. If the dolphin is your spirit animal, it might be a nudge to cultivate a more playful attitude and approach life with a sense of wonder.
- **Promoting Harmony and Cooperation:** Dolphins thrive in social pods, working together in harmony. The dolphin spirit animal encourages you to foster positive relationships, collaborate effectively with others, and promote peace and cooperation in your interactions.

Communication and Emotional Intelligence:

- **Clear and Effective Communication:** Dolphins are known for their complex communication system using clicks and whistles. The dolphin spirit animal reminds you to hone your communication skills, express yourself clearly, and listen actively to others.

- **Emotional Intelligence and Empathy:**
  Dolphins exhibit a high degree of emotional
  intelligence and empathy. This spirit animal
  encourages you to develop your emotional
  awareness, understand the feelings of others,
  and build meaningful connections.

Adaptability and Flow:

- **Graceful Navigation:** Dolphins move with
  incredible fluidity and grace through the water.
  This spirit animal signifies the importance of
  adapting to changing circumstances and
  navigating life's currents with ease and flexibility.
- **Going with the Flow:** The dolphin's playful spirit
  reminds you to trust the flow of life, embrace the
  present moment, and find joy in the journey
  itself.

The Shadow Side of the Dolphin:

While the dolphin's symbolism is largely positive, it's
important to consider some complexities:

- **Frivolousness and Superficiality:** The
  dolphin's emphasis on playfulness can
  sometimes manifest as a tendency towards
  frivolity or superficiality. The dolphin spirit animal
  reminds you to find a balance between joy and
  responsibility, and to pursue meaningful goals
  alongside moments of lightheartedness.
- **Fear of Facing Challenges:** The dolphin's
  preference for calm waters can represent a
  reluctance to face challenges or navigate difficult

emotions. The dolphin spirit animal encourages you to develop resilience and approach obstacles with courage and optimism.

A Messenger of Connection and Joy:

Ultimately, the dolphin spirit animal is a messenger of connection and joy. It encourages you to:

- **Embrace Playfulness:** Find moments of joy and cultivate a lighthearted approach to life.
- **Communicate Effectively:** Develop your communication skills and build strong relationships based on empathy and understanding.
- **Navigate with Grace:** Adapt to change with flexibility and navigate life's challenges with ease.
- **Go with the Flow:** Trust the natural flow of life, embrace the present moment, and find joy in the journey.

As you walk alongside this playful spirit guide, you learn to connect with others with joy, navigate life's currents with grace, and find your own unique rhythm of happiness and purpose.

Deer

The deer, a creature of elegance and grace with gentle eyes and swift movements, frequently appears as a spirit animal. Its symbolism is rich and multifaceted, offering valuable lessons about gentleness, intuition, renewal, and finding your path through life with a quiet strength.

Embracing Gentleness and Kindness:

- **Compassion and Empathy:** The deer embodies gentleness, kindness, and a compassionate nature. If the deer is your spirit animal, it might be a reminder to cultivate these qualities in your interactions with others and the world around you.
- **Inner Peace and Tranquility:** The deer's calm demeanor signifies the importance of inner peace and tranquility. This spirit animal encourages you to find ways to cultivate serenity amidst life's challenges.

Following Your Intuition and Inner Wisdom:

- **Sharpened Senses and Awareness:** Deers possess keen senses, particularly sight and hearing. The deer spirit animal reminds you to pay attention to your intuition and inner wisdom. Trust your gut feelings and hone your observational skills to navigate life's path.

- **Connecting with the Natural World:** Deers are often found in tranquil forests and meadows. This spirit animal signifies a deep connection with the natural world. Spend time in nature to find peace, inspiration, and a deeper connection to yourself.

Renewal and Rebirth:

- **New Beginnings and Fresh Starts:** Deers are known for their annually regrowing antlers, symbolizing renewal and rebirth. The deer spirit animal can represent a time for new beginnings, fresh starts, and personal growth.
- **Overcoming Challenges with Grace:** Deers are surprisingly resilient creatures, able to navigate challenging terrain with grace. This spirit animal encourages you to approach obstacles with courage and overcome them with dignity.

The Shadow Side of the Deer:

The deer's symbolism also carries some complexities:

- **Timidity and Shyness:** The deer's natural shyness can sometimes manifest as timidity or a reluctance to stand up for yourself. The deer spirit animal reminds you to develop your assertiveness while maintaining your gentle nature.
- **Fear and Indecision:** The deer's flight instinct can represent a tendency towards fear or indecision. This spirit animal encourages you to

trust your intuition, face your fears with courage, and make clear decisions.

A Messenger of Quiet Strength:

Ultimately, the deer spirit animal is a messenger of quiet strength. It encourages you to:

- **Embrace Gentleness:** Cultivate kindness, compassion, and a peaceful demeanor in your interactions with others.
- **Trust Your Intuition:** Honor your gut feelings and develop your intuition as a valuable guide.
- **Seek Renewal and Growth:** Embrace new beginnings and personal growth opportunities.
- **Face Challenges with Grace:** Approach obstacles with courage and overcome them with dignity.
- **Find Strength in Quiet Confidence:** Develop your inner strength and navigate life's path with quiet determination.

By understanding the symbolism of the deer, you gain valuable insights into your strengths and areas for growth. As you walk alongside this gentle spirit guide, you learn to navigate life with intuition, grace, and a quiet strength that allows you to overcome challenges and blossom into your full potential.

Tiger

The tiger, a majestic predator with a fiery spirit and a powerful presence, frequently appears as a spirit animal across many cultures. Its symbolism is rich and multifaceted, offering guidance on leadership, passion, courage, and embracing your inner strength to navigate life's challenges with unwavering determination.

Embracing Power and Leadership:

- **Strength and Confidence:** The tiger embodies immense physical and inner strength. If the tiger is your spirit animal, it might be a call to tap into your own leadership potential and approach life with unwavering confidence.
- **Fierce Protection:** Tigers are fiercely protective of their territory and young. The tiger spirit animal can represent a protective force, urging you to stand up for yourself and those you love.

Harnessing Passion and Drive:

- **Passion and Intensity:** The tiger's fiery spirit signifies a passionate and intense nature. This spirit animal encourages you to pursue your goals with unwavering determination and channel your passion into creative endeavors.
- **Embracing Your Wild Side:** The tiger's untamed nature represents a connection to your own wild side, your raw instincts, and a zest for

life. Don't be afraid to embrace your adventurous spirit and explore new experiences.

Developing Courage and Independence:

- **Confronting Fears:** Tigers are fearless hunters, taking on prey much larger than themselves. The tiger spirit animal encourages you to confront your fears with courage and overcome challenges that stand in your path.
- **Independent Spirit:** Solitary creatures by nature, tigers represent independence and self-reliance. You possess the strength and resourcefulness to navigate life's journey on your own terms.

The Shadow Side of the Tiger:

The tiger's symbolism also carries some complexities:

- **Recklessness and Aggression:** The tiger's fierce nature can sometimes manifest as recklessness, impulsivity, or an excess of aggression. The tiger spirit animal reminds you to channel your power with control and avoid unnecessary conflict.
- **Domination and Controlling Tendencies:** The tiger's dominance in its territory can represent a shadow aspect of controlling tendencies or a desire to dominate others. The tiger spirit animal encourages you to use your strength with respect and lead by inspiration, not intimidation.

A Messenger of Untamed Potential:

Ultimately, the tiger spirit animal is a messenger of untamed potential. It encourages you to:

- **Embrace Your Inner Strength:** Develop your leadership qualities, confidence, and unwavering determination.
- **Pursue Your Passions:** Channel your passion and intensity into achieving your goals and living a fulfilling life.
- **Conquer Your Fears:** Face challenges with courage and overcome obstacles that stand in your way.
- **Navigate Life with Independence:** Carve your own path and trust in your ability to navigate life on your own terms.
- **Lead with Inspiration:** Use your strength to inspire others and create positive change in the world.

By understanding the symbolism of the tiger, you gain valuable insights into your strengths and weaknesses. As you walk alongside this powerful spirit guide, you learn to harness your inner fire, navigate life's challenges with courage, and embrace your untamed potential to lead and create a life of passion and purpose.

Sloth

The sloth, an unusual creature known for its slow-moving lifestyle and laid-back demeanor, might not be the first animal that comes to mind as a spirit animal. However, beneath its seemingly sluggish exterior lies a wealth of symbolism offering valuable lessons about patience, conservation of energy, mindfulness, and appreciating the simple joys in life.

Embracing Patience and Acceptance:

- **Living in the Slow Lane:** The sloth's deliberate pace reminds us of the importance of slowing down and appreciating the present moment. If the sloth is your spirit animal, it might be a nudge to take a step back from the hustle and bustle of life and embrace patience in your endeavors.
- **Acceptance and Inner Peace:** The sloth's acceptance of its slow nature signifies the importance of finding inner peace and accepting things as they are. This spirit animal encourages you to let go of the need to control everything and trust in the natural flow of life.

Conservation of Energy and Resourcefulness:

- **Living Deliberately:** Sloths carefully ration their energy, moving only when necessary. The sloth spirit animal reminds you to be mindful of your energy expenditure and prioritize tasks that align with your values and goals.

- **Resourcefulness with Limited Means:** Despite their slowness, sloths have adapted to thrive in their environment. This spirit animal signifies the importance of being resourceful and finding creative solutions, even with limited means.

Mindfulness and Connection with Nature:

- **Present Moment Awareness:** Hanging upside down, sloths spend a significant amount of time simply observing their surroundings. The sloth spirit animal encourages you to cultivate mindfulness and appreciate the beauty of the world around you.
- **Connecting with the Natural World:** Sloths spend their entire lives in the trees, existing in harmony with nature. This spirit animal reminds you to nurture your connection with the natural world and find peace in spending time outdoors.

The Shadow Side of the Sloth:

The sloth's symbolism also carries some complexities:

- **Procrastination and Laziness:** The sloth's slowness can sometimes manifest as procrastination or a reluctance to take action. The sloth spirit animal reminds you to find a healthy balance between slowing down and taking initiative when needed.
- **Disengagement and Apathy:** In its shadow aspect, the sloth's laid-back nature can

represent a tendency towards disengagement or apathy. The sloth spirit animal encourages you to find a balance between relaxation and taking responsibility for your life.

A Messenger of Contentment and Inner Peace:

Ultimately, the sloth spirit animal is a messenger of contentment and inner peace. It encourages you to:

- **Embrace Slowness:** Slow down, appreciate the present moment, and avoid the pressure to constantly be on the go.
- **Prioritize Inner Peace:** Cultivate acceptance and find peace within yourself, regardless of external circumstances.
- **Be Mindful of Your Energy:** Be deliberate in your actions and prioritize tasks that align with your values.
- **Connect with Nature:** Spend time outdoors, appreciate the beauty of the natural world, and find peace in its serenity.
- **Find Joy in the Simple Things:** Slow down and appreciate the simple joys and wonders that life has to offer.

By understanding the symbolism of the sloth, you gain valuable insights into your approach to life and priorities. As you walk alongside this gentle spirit guide, you learn to embrace slowness, conserve your energy, and find contentment in the present moment.

Crow

The crow, a ubiquitous and intelligent bird often shrouded in myth and legend, frequently appears as a powerful spirit animal. Its symbolism is rich and multifaceted, encompassing wisdom, transformation, adaptability, and the ability to navigate between the physical and spiritual realms.

Embracing Wisdom and Insight:

- **Keeper of Secrets and Knowledge:** Crows have long been associated with wisdom and the possession of hidden knowledge. The crow spirit animal may be urging you to tap into your own intuition and inner wisdom.
- **Observation and Discernment:** Crows are highly observant creatures, adept at noticing details and patterns. This spirit animal encourages you to develop your observational skills and approach situations with discernment.

Transformation and Change:

- **Embracing Transitions:** Crows are known for their adaptability and ability to thrive in diverse environments. The crow spirit animal can be a messenger of change, urging you to embrace new beginnings and navigate life's transitions with grace.
- **Death and Rebirth:** In many cultures, crows are associated with death and the afterlife. The crow

spirit animal can symbolize transformation, reminding you that endings are often necessary for new beginnings.

Adaptability and Resourcefulness:

- **Problem-Solvers and Opportunists:** Crows are intelligent creatures, known for their problem-solving skills and ability to find food and resources. The crow spirit animal encourages you to be resourceful and find creative solutions to overcome challenges.
- **Thriving in Different Environments:** Crows can adapt to a variety of habitats. This spirit animal signifies the importance of being adaptable and flexible in your approach to life.

The Shadow Side of the Crow:

The crow's symbolism also carries some complexities:

- **Mischief and Deception:** The crow's intelligence can sometimes manifest as a tendency towards mischief or even deception. The crow spirit animal reminds you to act with integrity and avoid manipulating others.
- **Ill Omen and Negativity:** In some cultures, crows are seen as harbingers of bad luck or death. However, this association can also represent transformation and the need to let go of the past. The crow spirit animal encourages you to focus on the positive aspects of change and new beginnings.

A Messenger of Transformation and Hidden Knowledge:

Ultimately, the crow spirit animal is a messenger of transformation and hidden knowledge. It encourages you to:

- **Develop Your Intuition:** Tap into your inner wisdom and trust your gut feelings.
- **Embrace Change:** See transitions as opportunities for growth and new beginnings.
- **Be Resourceful and Adaptable:** Find creative solutions to overcome challenges and thrive in different situations.
- **Seek Hidden Knowledge:** Explore the world with curiosity and a thirst for knowledge.
- **Embrace the Mystery:** Acknowledge the mysteries of life and death, and find beauty in the unknown.

As you walk alongside this wise spirit guide, you learn to navigate life's changes with discernment, resourcefulness, and a connection to the unseen realms.

Coyote

The coyote, a cunning and adaptable creature often featured in myths and legends, holds a powerful presence as a spirit animal. Its symbolism is rich and multifaceted, encompassing playfulness, resourcefulness, creativity, and the ability to navigate life's challenges with cleverness and humor.

Embracing Playfulness and a Trickster Spirit:

- **Finding Joy and Laughter:** The coyote's playful nature embodies the importance of finding joy and humor in everyday life. If the coyote is your spirit animal, it might be a nudge to lighten up, embrace playfulness, and find laughter even amidst challenges.
- **The Trickster Archetype:** The coyote is often depicted as a trickster figure, using wit and cunning to overcome obstacles. The coyote spirit animal encourages you to embrace your creativity and find unconventional solutions to problems.

Resourcefulness and Adaptability:

- **Thriving in Tough Conditions:** Coyotes are highly adaptable creatures, able to survive in diverse and challenging environments. This spirit animal signifies the importance of being resourceful and finding ways to thrive with limited resources.

- **Thinking Outside the Box:** The coyote's cunning nature represents the ability to think outside the box and find creative solutions. The coyote spirit animal encourages you to approach problems from different angles and challenge the status quo.

The Shadow Side of the Coyote:

The coyote's symbolism also carries some complexities:

- **Deception and Mischief:** The coyote's trickster nature can sometimes manifest as a tendency towards deception or manipulation. The coyote spirit animal reminds you to use your cunning for good and avoid using it to harm others.
- **Recklessness and Impulsiveness:** The coyote's playful spirit can sometimes lead to recklessness or impulsiveness. The coyote spirit animal encourages you to balance your playful side with a sense of responsibility and consider the consequences of your actions.

A Messenger of Transformation and Creative Problem-Solving:

Ultimately, the coyote spirit animal is a messenger of transformation and creative problem-solving. It encourages you to:

- **Embrace Playfulness:** Find moments of joy and laughter in life, even during challenging times.

- **Think Creatively:** Approach problems from new angles and find unconventional solutions.
- **Be Resourceful and Adaptable:** Find ways to thrive in different situations and overcome obstacles with ingenuity.
- **Embrace the Trickster Spirit:** Use your wit and cunning for good, but act with integrity and avoid manipulation.
- **Learn from Your Mistakes:** Embrace the lessons learned from your mistakes and use them to grow as a person.

By understanding the symbolism of the coyote, you gain valuable insights into your strengths and areas for growth. As you walk alongside this trickster spirit guide, you learn to navigate life's challenges with playfulness, resourcefulness, and a touch of clever wit.

Butterfly

The butterfly, a captivating creature known for its breathtaking metamorphosis, frequently appears as a symbol of hope, transformation, and beauty. As a spirit animal, the butterfly carries a wealth of symbolism offering guidance on personal growth, embracing new beginnings, and finding joy in the simple beauty of life.

Embracing Transformation and Growth:

- **Metamorphosis as a Symbol:** The butterfly's incredible transformation from caterpillar to winged creature embodies the power of personal growth and change. If the butterfly is your spirit animal, it might be a sign that you're undergoing a period of significant transformation or are on the cusp of positive change.
- **Letting Go of the Past:** The chrysalis stage of the butterfly symbolizes shedding the limitations of the past. The butterfly spirit animal encourages you to release what no longer serves you and embrace new possibilities.

Finding Joy and Beauty:

- **Appreciating the Present Moment:** Butterflies flit from flower to flower, savoring the nectar of each moment. The butterfly spirit animal reminds you to slow down, appreciate the beauty around you, and find joy in the simple things.

- **Living a Life of Color and Vibrancy:** Butterflies come in a dazzling array of colors and patterns. This spirit animal encourages you to embrace your own unique qualities and express yourself with vibrancy and joy.

The Shadow Side of the Butterfly:

While the butterfly's symbolism is largely positive, there are some complexities to consider:

- **Fear of Change:** The dramatic transformation of the butterfly can represent a fear of change or the unknown. The butterfly spirit animal encourages you to embrace change as an opportunity for growth, not something to be feared.
- **Superficiality:** The butterfly's focus on beauty can sometimes manifest as superficiality or a preoccupation with appearances. The butterfly spirit animal reminds you to cultivate inner beauty and seek meaning beyond the surface.

A Messenger of Hope and Personal Growth:

Ultimately, the butterfly spirit animal is a messenger of hope and personal growth. It encourages you to:

- **Embrace Transformation:** See change as an opportunity to evolve into your best self.
- **Let Go of the Past:** Release what no longer serves you and open yourself to new beginnings.

- **Find Joy in the Present Moment:** Slow down, appreciate the beauty around you, and find joy in the simple things.
- **Embrace Your Vibrancy:** Express yourself with your unique colors and shine brightly in the world.
- **Seek Meaning Beyond Appearances:** Cultivate inner beauty and wholeness.

By understanding the symbolism of the butterfly, you gain valuable insights into your approach to change and your ability to find joy in life. As you walk alongside this transformative spirit guide, you learn to embrace personal growth, find beauty in the everyday, and spread your wings to experience the full potential of your colorful journey.

Elephant

The elephant, a majestic and intelligent creature revered in many cultures, holds a powerful presence as a spirit animal. Its symbolism is rich and multifaceted, offering guidance on strength, wisdom, loyalty, community, and remembering the importance of the past while forging your path forward.

Embracing Strength and Stability:

- **Inner Strength and Resilience:** The elephant's immense size and physical power embody inner strength, resilience, and the ability to overcome challenges. If the elephant is your spirit animal, it might be a reminder to tap into your own inner strength and face difficulties with unwavering determination.
- **Stability and Grounding:** Elephants are known for their stability and grounding presence. The elephant spirit animal encourages you to find your own sense of inner stability and remain grounded amidst life's uncertainties.

Wisdom and Memory:

- **Keeper of Knowledge and Traditions:** Elephants are highly intelligent creatures with excellent memories. The elephant spirit animal signifies the importance of wisdom gained through experience and honoring traditions that hold value.

- **Learning from the Past:** Elephants are known for their strong family bonds and passing down knowledge through generations. The elephant spirit animal encourages you to learn from your past experiences and the wisdom of those who came before you.

Loyalty and Community:

- **Fierce Protectors:** Elephants live in close-knit herds, fiercely protecting their young and each other. The elephant spirit animal signifies the importance of loyalty, family, and strong community bonds.
- **Compassion and Empathy:** Elephants exhibit empathy and compassion towards each other. This spirit animal encourages you to cultivate these qualities in your relationships and build a supportive network around you.

The Shadow Side of the Elephant:

The elephant's symbolism also carries some complexities:

- **Stubbornness and Resistance to Change:** The elephant's immense size can sometimes represent a tendency towards stubbornness or resistance to change. The elephant spirit animal reminds you to be flexible and open to new possibilities while maintaining your core values.
- **Destructive Power:** The elephant's immense strength can be destructive if not channeled properly. The elephant spirit animal encourages

you to use your strength for good and avoid using it to harm yourself or others.

A Messenger of Strength, Wisdom, and Community:

Ultimately, the elephant spirit animal is a messenger of strength, wisdom, and community. It encourages you to:

- **Embrace Your Inner Strength:** Develop your resilience and face challenges with unwavering determination.
- **Find Stability and Grounding:** Cultivate a sense of inner peace and remain grounded amidst life's uncertainties.
- **Seek and Share Knowledge:** Learn from your experiences and the wisdom of others, and share your knowledge to inspire others.
- **Nurture Loyalty and Community:** Build strong and supportive relationships based on loyalty, compassion, and empathy.
- **Use Your Strength for Good:** Channel your inner strength to make a positive impact on the world.

By understanding the symbolism of the elephant, you gain valuable insights into your strengths and areas for growth. As you walk alongside this wise and powerful spirit guide, you learn to navigate life with strength, wisdom, and a deep connection to your community and your roots.

Hawk

The hawk, a keen-eyed predator with a powerful presence, frequently appears as a spirit animal across many cultures. Its symbolism is rich and multifaceted, offering guidance on vision, focus, leadership, and achieving your goals with unwavering determination.

Sharp Vision and Observation:

- **Clarity and Insight:** The hawk's exceptional eyesight signifies the importance of clear vision and insight. If the hawk is your spirit animal, it might be a nudge to see situations with greater clarity and make well-informed decisions.
- **Developing Your Observational Skills:** Hawks meticulously observe their surroundings before striking. The hawk spirit animal encourages you to hone your observational skills, pick up on subtle details, and develop a deeper understanding of the world around you.

Focus and Determination:

- **Goal Setting and Achievement:** The hawk's relentless pursuit of prey embodies the importance of setting clear goals and pursuing them with unwavering focus. The hawk spirit animal encourages you to set ambitious goals and dedicate yourself to achieving them.
- **Overcoming Obstacles:** Hawks are skilled hunters, adept at navigating challenges to reach

their targets. The hawk spirit animal encourages you to develop the perseverance and determination to overcome obstacles on your path to success.

Leadership and Independence:

- **Taking Charge and Leading by Example:** Hawks are often solitary creatures at the top of the food chain. The hawk spirit animal signifies leadership potential and the ability to inspire others.
- **Independent Spirit and Self-Reliance:** Hawks are self-sufficient hunters, relying on their own skills to survive. The hawk spirit animal encourages you to cultivate independence, trust in your abilities, and carve your own path.

The Shadow Side of the Hawk:

The hawk's symbolism also carries some complexities:

- **Ruthlessness and Aggression:** The hawk's predatory nature can sometimes manifest as ruthlessness or excessive aggression. The hawk spirit animal reminds you to use your power with discernment and avoid harming others in your pursuit of goals.
- **Arrogance and Overconfidence:** The hawk's dominance can lead to arrogance or overconfidence. The hawk spirit animal reminds you to balance ambition with humility and acknowledge the strengths and perspectives of others.

A Messenger of Vision and Soaring Potential:

Ultimately, the hawk spirit animal is a messenger of vision and soaring potential. It encourages you to:

- **Develop Your Vision:** Set clear goals, cultivate a clear vision for your future, and see possibilities beyond limitations.
- **Focus and Determination:** Pursue your goals with unwavering focus, dedication, and perseverance.
- **Embrace Your Leadership Potential:** Develop your leadership skills and inspire others with your vision and determination.
- **Navigate Challenges with Grace:** Develop the resilience and resourcefulness to overcome obstacles on your path.
- **Find Balance in Power:** Use your strength and ambition with wisdom, compassion, and respect for others.

By understanding the symbolism of the hawk, you gain valuable insights into your strengths and areas for growth. As you walk alongside this powerful spirit guide, you learn to see the world with greater clarity, set ambitious goals, and soar high towards achieving your full potential.

Horse

The horse, a majestic and powerful creature with a rich history alongside humanity, frequently appears as a spirit animal across many cultures. Its symbolism is rich and multifaceted, offering guidance on freedom, strength, passion, forging strong partnerships, and journeying through life with grace and independence.

Embracing Freedom and Independence:

- **Untamed Spirit and Liberation:** The horse's wild spirit embodies the desire for freedom and independence. If the horse is your spirit animal, it might be a sign that you crave freedom in some aspect of your life.
- **Breaking Free from Limitations:** Horses are known for their powerful strides and ability to gallop across vast landscapes. The horse spirit animal encourages you to break free from limitations, fears, or restrictive situations that hold you back.

Strength and Power:

- **Inner Strength and Resilience:** The horse's physical strength and stamina represent inner fortitude and resilience. The horse spirit animal reminds you of your own inner strength and the ability to overcome challenges with determination.

- **Harnessing Your Power:** Horses are capable of great power and speed when directed with a gentle hand. The horse spirit animal encourages you to learn to harness your own power and channel it productively.

Passion and Zest for Life:

- **Following Your Passions:** Horses possess a natural zest for life and a willingness to run free. The horse spirit animal encourages you to identify your passions and pursue them with enthusiasm.
- **Embracing Adventure:** Horses are often associated with exploration and adventure. The horse spirit animal reminds you to embrace new experiences and approach life with a sense of adventure.

Partnership and Collaboration:

- **Building Strong Bonds:** Horses form deep bonds with their human companions, based on mutual trust and respect. The horse spirit animal signifies the importance of building strong and supportive partnerships in life.
- **Communication and Cooperation:** Horses communicate effectively with humans through body language and cues. The horse spirit animal encourages you to develop your communication skills and collaborate effectively with others.

The Shadow Side of the Horse:

The horse's symbolism also carries some complexities:

- **Stubbornness and Resistance:** Horses can be stubborn and resistant to direction if not handled with patience and understanding. The horse spirit animal reminds you to be flexible and adaptable while staying true to your core values.
- **Recklessness and Impulsivity:** The horse's powerful energy can sometimes lead to recklessness or impulsive decisions. The horse spirit animal encourages you to balance your adventurous spirit with a sense of responsibility and consider the consequences of your actions.

A Messenger of Freedom and Connection:

Ultimately, the horse spirit animal is a messenger of freedom and connection. It encourages you to:

- **Embrace Your Freedom:** Break free from limitations and pursue the life you desire.
- **Develop Your Inner Strength:** Cultivate your resilience and overcome challenges with determination.
- **Follow Your Passions:** Pursue your goals with enthusiasm and a zest for life.
- **Build Strong Partnerships:** Nurture supportive and trusting relationships with others.
- **Navigate Life with Grace and Independence:** Embrace your individuality while collaborating effectively with others on your journey.

By understanding the symbolism of the horse, you gain valuable insights into your strengths and areas for growth. As you walk alongside this powerful spirit guide, you learn to harness your inner strength, embrace your adventurous spirit, and forge meaningful connections as you journey through life with freedom and grace.

Owl

The owl, a nocturnal creature with keen eyesight and a silent flight, frequently appears as a powerful spirit animal across many cultures. Its symbolism is rich and multifaceted, offering guidance on wisdom, intuition, discernment, seeing beyond the surface, and navigating life's mysteries with insight and understanding.

Embracing Wisdom and Knowledge:

- **Keeper of Secrets and Ancient Knowledge:** Owls have long been associated with wisdom and the possession of hidden knowledge. The owl spirit animal may be urging you to tap into your own intuition and inner wisdom.
- **Seeing Beyond the Obvious:** Owls have exceptional night vision, allowing them to see clearly in darkness. The owl spirit animal encourages you to develop your discernment, look beyond surface appearances, and perceive the deeper truths in situations.

Intuition and the Unseen:

- **Trusting Your Gut:** Owls are highly attuned to their surroundings and rely heavily on intuition. The owl spirit animal encourages you to trust your intuition and gut feelings, as they may be guiding you in the right direction.

- **Exploring the Mysteries of Life:** Owls are often associated with magic and the unseen realms. The owl spirit animal signifies the importance of exploring the mysteries of life and the universe with an open mind.

Adaptability and Resourcefulness:

- **Thriving in the Dark:** Owls are perfectly adapted to their nocturnal environment. The owl spirit animal signifies the importance of being adaptable and resourceful, even in challenging situations.
- **Silent Observation:** Owls observe their surroundings silently before striking. The owl spirit animal encourages you to be a keen observer, gather information before acting, and make well-informed decisions.

The Shadow Side of the Owl:

The owl's symbolism also carries some complexities:

- **Isolation and Loneliness:** Owls are often solitary creatures. The owl spirit animal may be a sign that you crave solitude or might be feeling isolated. However, it can also encourage you to find a balance between solitude and social connection.
- **Fear of the Unknown:** The owl's association with darkness can sometimes represent a fear of the unknown or unseen. The owl spirit animal encourages you to confront your fears and embrace the mysteries of life with courage.

A Messenger of Insight and Hidden Wisdom:

Ultimately, the owl spirit animal is a messenger of insight and hidden wisdom. It encourages you to:

- **Develop Your Intuition:** Trust your gut feelings and inner knowing.
- **See Beyond Appearances:** Look deeper to understand the underlying truths in situations.
- **Embrace the Mysteries:** Explore the unseen realms and the mysteries of life with an open mind.
- **Be a Wise Observer:** Gather information, observe carefully, and make well-informed decisions.
- **Embrace Solitude in Balance:** Find a healthy balance between solitude for reflection and connection with others.

By understanding the symbolism of the owl, you gain valuable insights into your strengths and areas for growth. As you walk alongside this wise spirit guide, you learn to navigate life's mysteries with discernment, tap into your intuition, and find wisdom in the hidden knowledge that surrounds you.

Lion

The lion, a majestic predator with a powerful presence, frequently appears as a spirit animal across many cultures. Its symbolism is rich and multifaceted, offering guidance on courage, leadership, strength, self-confidence, and taking action to create the life you desire.

Embracing Courage and Bravery:

- **Facing Challenges with Fearlessness:** The lion's bravery in hunting and defending its territory embodies the importance of facing challenges with courage. If the lion is your spirit animal, it might be a sign that you need to step outside your comfort zone and conquer your fears.
- **Inner Strength and Determination:** The lion's imposing physique represents immense inner strength and unwavering determination. The lion spirit animal encourages you to tap into your own inner strength and face life's obstacles with determination.

Leadership and Taking Charge:

- **Natural Leader and Inspiration:** Lions live in prides with a social hierarchy, with the lioness leading the hunt and the male lion protecting the pride. The lion spirit animal signifies leadership potential and the ability to inspire others.

- **Taking Responsibility and Ownership:** As the leader of the pride, the lion takes responsibility for the well-being of the group. The lion spirit animal encourages you to take charge of your life, make decisions, and own your actions.

Confidence and Self-Esteem:

- **Believing in Yourself:** The lion's regal presence signifies self-confidence and a strong sense of self-worth. The lion spirit animal encourages you to believe in yourself, your abilities, and your potential to achieve your goals.
- **Standing Up for Yourself:** Lions are fearless in defending themselves and their pride. The lion spirit animal reminds you to stand up for yourself, your values, and what you believe in.

The Shadow Side of the Lion:

The lion's symbolism also carries some complexities:

- **Arrogance and Domination:** The lion's dominance within its pride can sometimes manifest as arrogance or a tendency to control others. The lion spirit animal reminds you to use your strength with compassion and lead by inspiration, not intimidation.
- **Recklessness and Impulsivity:** A lion's hunting instincts can lead to recklessness or impulsive actions. The lion spirit animal encourages you to balance your courage with strategic thinking and avoid making choices based solely on impulse.

A Messenger of Strength and Taking Action:

Ultimately, the lion spirit animal is a messenger of strength and taking action. It encourages you to:

- **Embrace Your Courage:** Face your fears, conquer challenges, and step outside your comfort zone.
- **Develop Your Leadership Potential:** Lead by example, inspire others, and take responsibility for your actions.
- **Cultivate Confidence:** Believe in yourself, your abilities, and your worth.
- **Stand Up for Your Values:** Have the courage to defend what you believe in.
- **Act with Strength and Compassion:** Use your power for good and lead with empathy and understanding.

By understanding the symbolism of the lion, you gain valuable insights into your strengths and areas for growth. As you walk alongside this regal spirit guide, you learn to develop your courage, embrace your leadership potential, and confidently stride towards achieving your goals.

Rabbit

The rabbit, a quick and adaptable creature often featured in myths and folklore, holds a significant presence as a spirit animal. Its symbolism is rich and multifaceted, offering guidance on resourcefulness, creativity, intuition, alertness, and embracing new beginnings with a touch of caution.

Adaptability and Resourcefulness:

- **Thriving in Different Environments:** Rabbits can adapt to diverse habitats, from deserts to forests. The rabbit spirit animal signifies the importance of being resourceful and finding ways to thrive in different situations.
- **Thinking Outside the Box:** Rabbits are known for their cleverness and ability to outsmart predators. The rabbit spirit animal encourages you to think creatively, find unconventional solutions, and overcome challenges with ingenuity.

Intuition and Alertness:

- **Trusting Your Gut:** Rabbits rely heavily on their senses and intuition to avoid danger. The rabbit spirit animal encourages you to trust your gut feelings and pay attention to your intuition, as it may be guiding you in the right direction.
- **Staying Alert and Aware:** Rabbits are constantly aware of their surroundings. The

rabbit spirit animal reminds you to stay alert, be perceptive of your environment, and pick up on subtle cues.

New Beginnings and Fertility:

- **Embracing Fresh Starts:** Rabbits are known for their rapid reproduction, symbolizing new beginnings and fertility. The rabbit spirit animal may be a sign that a new chapter is unfolding in your life, filled with exciting possibilities.
- **Fertility and Abundance:** In many cultures, rabbits are associated with fertility and abundance. The rabbit spirit animal can represent new opportunities, growth, and prosperity coming your way.

The Shadow Side of the Rabbit:

The rabbit's symbolism also carries some complexities:

- **Fearfulness and Timidity:** Rabbits are naturally cautious creatures, quick to flee from danger. The rabbit spirit animal may be a sign that you are experiencing fear or anxiety. It encourages you to confront your fears and develop your courage.
- **Superficiality and Fickleness:** In some cultures, the rabbit is associated with being flighty or superficial. The rabbit spirit animal reminds you to focus on substance over appearances and to see things through before giving up.

A Messenger of Resourcefulness and New Beginnings:

Ultimately, the rabbit spirit animal is a messenger of resourcefulness and new beginnings. It encourages you to:

- **Embrace Your Resourcefulness:** Find creative solutions to overcome challenges and thrive in different situations.
- **Trust Your Intuition:** Pay attention to your gut feelings and inner knowing.
- **Stay Alert and Aware:** Be observant of your surroundings and pick up on important cues.
- **Embrace New Beginnings:** See change as an opportunity for growth and exciting new possibilities.
- **Confront Your Fears:** Develop your courage and face challenges with confidence.

By understanding this nimble spirit guide, you learn to navigate life's uncertainties with resourcefulness, embrace new beginnings with a cautious optimism, and find creative solutions to overcome any obstacle.

Orca

The orca, also known as the killer whale, is a majestic and intelligent creature that reigns supreme in the ocean depths. As a spirit animal, the orca carries powerful symbolism associated with community, communication, protection, powerful emotions, and navigating life's currents with grace and strength.

Community and Communication:

- **Strength in Numbers:** Orcas live in close-knit pods, working together to hunt and raise their young. The orca spirit animal signifies the importance of community, cooperation, and finding strength in unity.
- **Effective Communication:** Orcas use a complex system of vocalizations to communicate with each other. The orca spirit animal encourages you to develop your communication skills, express yourself clearly, and listen attentively to others.

Protection and Fierce Loyalty:

- **Guardians of the Ocean:** Orcas are apex predators, playing a vital role in maintaining the balance of the marine ecosystem. The orca spirit animal signifies fierce protectiveness and a willingness to defend those you care about.
- **Strong Family Bonds:** Orca pods are known for their strong family bonds, with mothers

fiercely protecting their calves. The orca spirit animal represents loyalty, devotion, and the importance of nurturing your loved ones.

Powerful Emotions and Intuition:

- **Emotional Depth and Sensitivity:** Orcas are believed to be highly intelligent creatures with a complex range of emotions. The orca spirit animal encourages you to embrace your emotional depth and express your feelings in a healthy way.
- **Intuition and Following Your Instincts:** Orcas are adept at navigating the vast oceans using their intuition. The orca spirit animal reminds you to trust your gut feelings and follow your instincts, especially when making important decisions.

The Shadow Side of the Orca:

The orca's symbolism also carries some complexities:

- **Destructive Power:** The orca's immense strength and hunting prowess can sometimes manifest as destructive tendencies. The orca spirit animal reminds you to use your power responsibly and avoid using it to harm others or the environment.
- **Shadowy Depths and Unconscious Emotions:** The orca's habitat in the ocean depths can represent the unconscious aspects of your psyche. The orca spirit animal may be

urging you to explore your hidden emotions and bring them to light.

A Messenger of Strength and Community:

Ultimately, the orca spirit animal is a messenger of strength, community, and navigating life's currents with grace. It encourages you to:

- **Value Your Community:** Build strong and supportive relationships with those who share your values.
- **Communicate Effectively:** Express yourself clearly, listen attentively, and bridge understanding.
- **Embrace Your Protective Instincts:** Fiercely defend those you care about and stand up for what you believe in.
- **Connect with Your Emotions:** Acknowledge your feelings, express them healthily, and trust your intuition.
- **Navigate Life's Currents with Strength:** Face challenges with determination, overcome obstacles, and move through life with grace and power.

By understanding the symbolism of the orca, you gain valuable insights into your strengths and areas for growth. As you walk alongside this powerful spirit guide, you learn to navigate life's currents with the support of your community, communicate effectively, and use your strength for protection and positive change.

Swan

The swan, a majestic and elegant bird often featured in myths and folklore, holds a powerful presence as a spirit animal. Its symbolism is rich and multifaceted, offering guidance on grace, beauty, transformation, new beginnings, and finding your voice.

Embracing Grace and Beauty:

- **Inner and Outer Beauty:** Swans are admired for their outward elegance and beauty. The swan spirit animal may be a sign to nurture your inner beauty as well, through kindness, compassion, and cultivating a positive attitude.
- **Moving Through Life with Poise:** Swans glide effortlessly across the water, symbolizing grace and poise. The swan spirit animal encourages you to move through life's challenges with elegance and composure.

Transformation and New Beginnings:

- **Metamorphosis from Ugly Duckling to Swan:** The swan's transformation from a clumsy duckling to a graceful adult represents the potential for profound personal growth. The swan spirit animal signifies that you are undergoing or are about to undergo a significant transformation.
- **Embracing New Chapters:** Swans migrate long distances, signifying new beginnings and

transitions. The swan spirit animal may be a message to embrace a new chapter in your life, letting go of the past and stepping into something exciting.

Finding Your Voice and Creativity:

- **Expressing Yourself Authentically:** Swans are known for their beautiful songs, particularly the male swan's loud trumpeting call. The swan spirit animal encourages you to find your voice, express yourself authentically, and share your unique gifts with the world.
- **Embracing Your Creative Potential:** Swans are sometimes depicted with feathers associated with music and poetry. The swan spirit animal may be urging you to explore your creative potential and express yourself through art, music, or writing.

The Shadow Side of the Swan:

The swan's symbolism also carries some complexities:

- **Vanity and Arrogance:** The swan's beauty can sometimes lead to vanity or a sense of superiority. The swan spirit animal reminds you to stay humble, appreciate the beauty in others, and avoid arrogance.
- **Hiding Your True Self:** Swans can appear graceful on the surface but can be aggressive when protecting their young. The swan spirit animal may be a sign that you are hiding your

true feelings or protecting yourself from getting hurt.

A Messenger of Graceful Transformation:

Ultimately, the swan spirit animal is a messenger of graceful transformation and finding your voice. It encourages you to:

- **Embrace Your Inner and Outer Beauty:** Cultivate kindness, compassion, and a positive attitude to radiate inner beauty.
- **Move Through Life with Grace:** Navigate challenges with poise and composure.
- **Embrace Transformation and New Beginnings:** See change as an opportunity for growth and exciting new possibilities.
- **Find Your Voice:** Express yourself authentically and share your unique gifts with the world.
- **Explore Your Creativity:** Embrace your creative potential and find ways to express yourself artistically.

By understanding the symbolism of the swan, you gain valuable insights into your strengths and areas for growth. As you walk alongside this graceful spirit guide, you learn to navigate life's transitions with elegance, find the courage to express yourself truly, and embark on a journey of beautiful transformation.

Whale

The whale, a majestic and enigmatic creature of the deep, holds a powerful presence as a spirit animal across many cultures. Its symbolism is rich and multifaceted, offering guidance on emotions, communication, community, intuition, and navigating the vast oceans of life with wisdom and grace.

Exploring the Depths of Your Emotions:

- **Connecting with Your Inner World:** Whales are known for their complex songs and vocalizations, believed to express a range of emotions. The whale spirit animal encourages you to explore the depths of your own emotions, understand their source, and express them healthily.
- **Intuition and Inner Knowing:** Whales navigate vast oceans using their intuition. The whale spirit animal reminds you to trust your gut feelings and inner knowing, as they may be guiding you in the right direction.

Communication and Building Strong Bonds:

- **The Power of Empathic Communication:** Whales use complex vocalizations to communicate with each other across vast distances. The whale spirit animal signifies the importance of empathic communication, listening deeply to others, and fostering strong connections.

- **Building Strong Communities:** Whales often live in close-knit pods, working together and supporting each other. The whale spirit animal encourages you to value your community, build strong relationships, and collaborate for a greater good.

Wisdom and Ancient Knowledge:

- **Keepers of the Deep:** Whales have inhabited the oceans for millions of years, holding a deep understanding of the natural world. The whale spirit animal signifies wisdom, knowledge of the cycles of life, and a connection to something ancient and profound.
- **Following Your Intuition and Inner Compass:** Whales navigate vast oceans using a combination of their senses and intuition. The whale spirit animal reminds you to trust your inner compass and follow your intuition, especially when making important decisions.

The Shadow Side of the Whale:

The whale's symbolism also carries some complexities:

- **Feeling Lost or Overwhelmed:** Getting lost in the vast ocean can represent feeling overwhelmed or lost in life's currents. The whale spirit animal may be a sign to seek guidance, connect with your support system, and navigate challenges with a clear direction.

- **Difficulty Expressing Emotions:** Whales communicate through complex sounds that humans may not fully understand. The whale spirit animal may be urging you to find healthy ways to express your emotions and be vulnerable with trusted loved ones.

A Messenger of Deep Wisdom and Connection:

Ultimately, the whale spirit animal is a messenger of deep wisdom, emotional connection, and navigating life's vast journeys with grace. It encourages you to:

- **Explore Your Emotional Depths:** Connect with your emotions, understand their source, and express them authentically.
- **Communicate with Empathy:** Listen deeply to others, express yourself clearly, and build strong connections.
- **Value Your Community:** Nurture your relationships, collaborate with others, and contribute to a greater good.
- **Embrace Your Intuition:** Trust your gut feelings and inner knowing as they guide you on your path.
- **Navigate Life with Wisdom:** Seek knowledge, learn from the past, and make choices that align with your values.

By understanding the symbolism of the whale, you gain valuable insights into your strengths and areas for growth. As you walk alongside this wise and powerful spirit guide, you learn to communicate effectively, connect deeply with your emotions and others, and navigate the vast oceans of life with wisdom, grace, and a sense of belonging.

The Journey Continues

Throughout this exploration, you've delved into the rich history and symbolism of spirit animals, learning the diverse methods to connect with them. Perhaps you've encountered these powerful guides through vivid dreams, meditative journeys, or felt an instant connection while researching a particular creature. Maybe your search is still unfolding, a patient wait for a sign or a deeper understanding.

The important thing to remember is that finding your spirit animals is a lifelong exploration, not a race to the finish line. As you navigate new experiences, your connection with these guides may deepen and evolve. Trust your intuition – it's the most crucial tool in this journey. Pay attention to recurring dreams, unexpected encounters with specific animals, or emotions evoked by different creatures in your research.

The process of connecting with your spirit animals is just as important as the destination itself. Embrace the journey, be patient, open yourself to new experiences, and trust that the right guides will reveal themselves when the time is right. Don't limit yourself to traditional interpretations – your spirit animals may not be the most obvious choices. Be open to unexpected connections and trust your gut feeling.

The concept of spirit animals is deeply rooted in respecting and honoring the natural world. Learn about the animals you connect with, appreciate their place in the ecosystem, and foster a connection with the environment. Remember, your spirit animals offer guidance and support, but ultimately, you are the author of your own story. Use their wisdom to navigate life's challenges, but don't become dependent on them.

Connecting with others who share an interest in spirit animals can be a source of inspiration and support. Share your experiences, insights, and interpretations with like-minded individuals. Finding your spirit animals is a transformative experience, a chance to connect with the deeper currents of your being and the natural world around you.

As you move forward, remember that your spirit guides are always present, offering their wisdom and strength to support you on your life's journey. Trust the path, embrace the unknown, and allow yourself to be guided by the magic of the animal kingdom. The adventure continues!

Did you find a powerful connection with a Spirit Animal? Share your thoughts and help others find their way!

Scan the QR code to leave a review for Spirit Animals

Preview The New Book By

Sarah Ripley

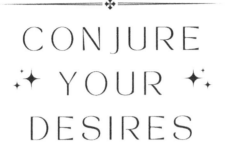

Sarah Ripley

Manifesting with Rituals, Spells, and Runes

Deep within us lies an innate power to shape our reality, a power harnessed by ancient pagans through rituals, spells, and the wisdom of nature. This book invites you to rediscover this magic, offering a practical guide to manifesting your heart's desires using timeless tools and techniques.

Step onto your path of magical creation with the foundational knowledge of establishing a sacred altar, your personal space for connecting with the unseen forces. Delve into the enchanting world of crystals, runes, and herbs, unlocking their unique properties and how they can amplify your intentions. Learn the language of the candles, letting their vibrant hues illuminate your desires and empower your rituals.

Harness the celestial rhythm of the moon, aligning your manifestations with the waxing and waning phases for optimal results. As you turn the pages, you'll encounter a wealth of powerful rituals and spells, designed to attract love, prosperity, healing, and more. Each practice is presented with clear instructions, making them accessible to both seasoned practitioners and curious beginners.

This book is not merely a collection of recipes; it's an invitation to embark on a personal journey of self-discovery and empowerment. As you engage with the practices within, you'll cultivate your intuition, refine your focus, and learn to harness the abundance of the universe. Remember, the most potent ingredient is your own belief, fueled by passion and purpose.

Whether you seek to nurture your creativity, attract abundance, or cultivate deeper self-love, this book serves as your guide, reminding you that the magic to manifest your desires lies within, waiting to be awakened. Let this journey empower you to rewrite your story, one intention, one ritual, one spell at a time.

About the Author

Sarah Ripley is a certified Life Coach, mentor, and author of books and journals on Numerology, Spirituality, Ancient Practices and Natural Healing. She is also a trained Chakra healer, Green Witch, and Master Herbalist.

Sarah has a passion for helping others to live their best lives. She believes that we all have the power to heal ourselves and create the life we want. Her work is focused on helping people to connect with their inner wisdom and intuition, and to develop the tools and skills they need to live their lives in alignment with their values and purpose.

Sarah has traveled throughout Asia, South America and Europe studying different cultures and spiritual beliefs. She is also a nature lover who has done extensive trekking in the Himalayas, Rockies and Andes Mountains. She is a passionate advocate for natural living and enjoys cooking with a completely natural diet. She spends her free time relaxing with her family and cats.

Sarah has been married for 28 years and has 2 adult children. She currently lives in Southeast Asia with her husband and 4 adopted street cats, where she continues to write, teach, and mentor others. She is also working on a new book about her experiences with natural healing and spirituality.

Made in the USA
Las Vegas, NV
08 April 2024

88402113R00079